PUBLIC
SERVICE
VALUES

PUBLIC SERVICE VALUES

RICHARD C. BOX

Routledge
Taylor & Francis Group

LONDON AND NEW YORK

First published 2014 by M.E. Sharpe

Published 2015 by Routledge
2 Park Square, Milton Park, Abingdon, Oxon OX14 4RN
711 Third Avenue, New York, NY 10017, USA

Routledge is an imprint of the Taylor & Francis Group, an informa business

Notices
No responsibility is assumed by the publisher for any injury and/or damage to
persons or property as a matter of products liability, negligence or otherwise,
or from any use of operation of any methods, products, instructions or ideas
contained in the material herein.

Practitioners and researchers must always rely on their own experience and
knowledge in evaluating and using any information, methods, compounds, or
experiments described herein. In using such information or methods they should
be mindful of their own safety and the safety of others, including parties for
whom they have a professional responsibility.

Product or corporate names may be trademarks or registered trademarks, and
are used only for identification and explanation without intent to infringe.

Library of Congress Cataloging-in-Publication Data

ISBN 13: 9780765643650 (pbk)
ISBN 13: 9780765643643 (hbk)

Contents

Foreword   ix

Preface   xv

1. The Public Professional and Public Service Values   3

The Importance of Values in the Public Sector   3

A Focus on the Public Professional   7

A Specific Sort of Values   11

Development of the Context of Public Service   15

Five Value Themes in Public Service   18

2. Public Service Values Today   22

Sources of Public Service Values   22

Studies of Public Service Values   23

Value Typologies   27

Values and Administrative Ethics   30

Democracy as a Source of Values   32

Codes of Ethics as a Source of Values   37

Public Service Values in Accreditation Standards   41

Using Values in the Five Thematic Chapters   43

Appendix A: Value Definitions from
Molina and McKeown   43

Appendix B: Practices to Promote the
ASPA Code of Ethics   46

**3. Neutrality: The Public Professional in a
Democratic Society**   51

The Idea of Neutrality in Public Service   51

Distinguishing Between Politics and Administration   54

Boundaries Around Daily Practice 59
Challenges to Neutrality 65
Values Associated with Neutrality 68
Applying Neutrality in Professional Life 71

4. **Efficiency: The Economic Environment of Public Service** 73
Efficiency as a Primary Value 73
Private Interest and Public Purpose 74
How Efficiency Became so Important 78
Beyond NPM 83
What Is Gained and What Is Lost: The Case of
    Vacation Beach 85
Values Associated with Efficiency 90
Applying Efficiency in Professional Life 93

5. **Accountability: Whom Do I Serve, and for What Purposes?** 95
Types of Accountability 95
Lawfulness as a Key Element of Accountability 98
Accountability to Elected Leaders and
    Organizational Superiors 100
Accountability to Citizens 104
Professional Accountability 107
The Public Interest as a Source of Accountability 110
Values Associated with Accountability 112
Applying Accountability in Professional Life 115

6. **Public Service: The Personal Commitment** 117
Core Elements of Public Service 117
The Environment of Professional Public Service 119
Professional Integrity and the Case of Park Woods 130
Making a Difference: The Public Professional as
    Agent of Change 135
Values Associated with Public Service 140
Applying the Value of Public Service in
    Professional Life 141

7. The Public Interest: Commitment to Society   144

The Meaning of Public Interest   144

Participativeness: The Public Interest over Time   147

Representativeness: Imagining the Public Interest   150

Transparency: Providing Full Information   152

Values Associated with Public Interest   155

Applying the Value of Public Interest in
Professional Life   161

**8. Conclusion: Value Choices and the Public
Professional**   163

Values in Practice   163

Imagination, Empathy, and the Public Interest   164

Public Service Values Across Cultures   164

Questions About Public Service Values in Practice   165

References   169

Index   175

About the Author   179

Foreword

Public Service Values reminds us that the founders of our nation and later the founders of our discipline placed strong emphasis on "regime values." For them, these values were the heart and soul of the discipline and professions we now call public affairs. They almost certainly would be disappointed to learn that these regime values are frequently conspicuous by their absence in public affairs courses and scholarship.

Public service values are rarely explicit in public affairs unless the topic is ethics—and ethics courses are not core courses in most MPA programs. It is as if we are afraid to engage these values openly in our classrooms and research for fear we will be judged less than rigorous and/or "emotional" as opposed to the more esteemed "rational."

When discussing the core functions of public organizations (e.g., budget and finance, human resource management, and strategic planning), public service values are at best a vague, amorphous, feel-good backdrop. They are not used to provoke discussion about which values might be relevant to core public functions and what aspects of administering these areas might elicit value conflicts for public professionals.

Public Service Values provides an opportunity for us to remedy these omissions in our teaching and research. Richard C. Box invites us to proudly and explicitly explore public service values as they apply to the decisions, dilemmas, actions, and choices of public professionals in the performance of their daily responsibilities.

This book is well grounded in the literature and in practice. The tone is bright, upbeat, and realistic; the analysis is rigorous and well documented. Also, if a passion for public service and a desire to support public professionals is "emotional," I am fine with the label and applaud the author's commitment. As a practitioner, I would argue that the author's explication of the values throughout the book as they apply to public professionals and their work is satisfyingly realistic and useful. "Rational" does not seem like a useful measure after noting these contributions of the book.

Public Service Values consists of eight chapters—five of which are devoted to the five value "themes" or "concepts," each of which encompasses many other related values. The themes are neutrality, efficiency, accountability, public service, and public interest. As a public professional, I found these five themes quite relevant to my experience and the parsing of each edifying and thought-provoking. I wish I had this book in my library when I was working in government.

A major strength of this book is its relentless focus on the individual public professional—on how she or he can use values as effective tools in daily work. The author reinforces this focus throughout the book—most notably at the end of his five theme chapters—with case examples and a final section on applying the value theme to professional life. The case examples stimulate reflection about what values are in play and challenge public professionals to be very deliberate when deciding what tradeoffs to make. The sections on applying values to professional life summarize the chapter's message about what each specific value cluster means for the public professional—how it fits in the current context, what values conflict, what values might take precedence.

Another major contribution of this book is the last chapter, in which the author provides an approach to holding ourselves as public service professionals accountable. He poses seven questions about public service values that, if used routinely, would contribute, as the author hopes, to "a more conscious and reflective public practice" and also enrich the professional lives of public professionals. Here are the seven questions:

1. Whom do I serve and for what purposes?
2. What is my personal relation to what I know?

3. What public service values are emphasized in the particular decision, event, policy, or practice that I am thinking about today?
4. What values are slighted or minimized in a particular situation that might be important to the people involved, to outcomes, and to future conditions?
5. Can I improve on my understanding of the circumstances surrounding a particular situation by using imagination and empathy?
6. Given what I know about public service values, are there policies, practices, or programs that might be changed in ways that better serve the values I think are important?
7. Am I acting in ways that will serve the public interest in the long term—for example, improving quality of life, social equity, and the condition of the natural environment?

These are questions that every aspiring public service professional should be taught to use and that current public service professionals should be strongly encouraged to make a habit of employing routinely.

As to what role this book should play in public affairs education, the author says the book is designed to be used "as a supplemental text for undergraduate or graduate courses in public affairs." I agree but think it has the potential to be useful well beyond such a modest scope.

Public Service Values challenges us to include public service values in our public affairs curricula, especially at the graduate level. As noted above, we give lip service to these values as we guide students through their programs, but we do little to help them understand what those values are. We also do little to help students determine for themselves which of the values they personally find most compelling and how to apply public service values in professional settings.

This neglect of explicit use of public service values across our curricula has significant costs. We may lose students who come to us passionate about public service, or, perhaps worse, we may quash the passion they bring to the program. We also miss the opportunity to prepare students much more completely for professional public service roles. If we do not stress public service values in their formal education, how will they know to invoke them in their professional roles?

Two stories support the above contentions: Years ago I met a newly minted MPA and asked him about his experience in the program he had just completed. His response: "I enrolled because I had a passion for public service and couldn't wait to get the skills and get out there and make a difference. I got no reinforcement of my passion during my program. In fact, I heard a lot of government bashing, even from some of my professors. It was more than disappointing."

More recently, I had a dual degree student (social work/MPA) in my intro class tell me his view of public administration: "It has no soul." He was quite angry at the time and said he was going to drop the MPA part of his degree and pursue only the social work master's, because he felt there was a lot of "soul" in social work.

These stories stayed with me because I felt that we in public affairs education had failed these students and probably many others who did not speak up. And the stories stayed with me because I believe there is plenty of "soul" in public affairs and in public service, but we have hidden it in a desperate attempt to be accepted in an instrumental world.

I think we need a balance in our curricula. Of course, we need to make sure our students acquire the skills they need to deal with the nuts and bolts of public organizations. As important, we need to ensure they understand and have struggled with the "soul" of public affairs and public service. The latter is much more difficult than the former. We are not doing our jobs as educators if we are not preparing our students for the messy, conflict-full environments they will be working in. We also are not doing our jobs if we do not reinforce and/or stimulate their passion for public service.

Public Service Values gives us an opportunity to meet these needs by returning to our roots. If we are serious about weaving public service values through our entire curriculum and making them once again the heart and soul of public affairs, this book can help us do that.

A bold approach to good use of this book in MPA programs would be to require all students to add it to their library at the beginning of their program. MPA faculty could then use the book as a supplemental text for all of their core courses. *Public Service Values* could be used in the introductory course to inform students about the "soul" of public affairs and public service. In the intro course they could also be told that the book will be a resource in all of their core courses and some of their electives (i.e., don't sell it!). Then, for each core course, faculty could refer students to the book to identify the public service contexts of the functions discussed in the course. For example, faculty teaching a basic budget and finance course might assign an exercise where the students need to consult the book to identify the public service context of budget development and the relevant public service values. Students would also answer the questions at the end of the book with budget development as the focus.

Public Service Values is a finely honed and inspiring gift to all of us in public affairs. It is now up to us to use it to restore public service values to their proper position in our classrooms and research. I suspect we all agree they are the heart and soul of our work. Let us act on that belief and use this book to explicitly discuss public service values in all core MPA courses and thereby give voice to the soul of our profession and discipline. By so doing we can revive our own passion for public service and reinforce the passion many of our students bring to their studies. And we can reinforce John Kirlin's view of public service in *Public Administration Review* (2001) as "a central part of the grandest of human endeavors—shaping a better future for ourselves and those yet unborn."

Mary R. Hamilton, PhD, CAE
Fellow, National Academy of Public Administration
Senior Executive in Residence,
University of Nebraska Omaha School of Public Administration

Preface

Values are not everything we need to know about why public professionals do what they do. We also need to know about political and economic conditions, legal and institutional constraints, professional ethics, and other influences that shape decisions and actions. Also, values are difficult to define, and the extent to which they implicitly or explicitly affect professional work is not easily measured. Despite these limitations, values are a powerful way to examine administrative behavior, and they provide a useful tool for professionals in daily practice.

This seems like a good time to focus on values in public service. The public sector has experienced waves of reform intended to make it more efficient, and the surrounding societal environment is often challenging, even hostile. At such a time, renewed attention to the purposes of professional work in public affairs seems appropriate in supporting understanding and effectiveness; *Public Service Values* is designed to contribute to this effort. It is not so much an exercise in research as it is a discussion of values that have been prominent in public administration for many decades and continue to be central to the work of students and practitioners of public service.

The reader familiar with administrative ethics will immediately recognize parallels between *Public Service Values* and texts on ethics. This is unavoidable, since the study of administrative ethics is also the study of values underlying ethical choice, but here we concentrate on the values themselves rather than the process of ethical decision making. As in administrative ethics, the "unit of analysis" is the individual public professional, in contrast to the framework of systems and political oversight of administrative agencies often found in writing on public affairs. The public service values approach allows us to explore the meaning and usefulness of specific values, making them more accessible as part of the workplace tool kit of people delivering public services.

This focus on the individual public service practitioner is evident from the substance of the chapters in *Public Service Values*. Five primary concepts, or themes, are used as an organizing framework for discussion of a range of values people in the field find important in their work. Other concepts could have been used and might serve the purpose equally well. These five were chosen because they align with central issues discussed in the research literature of public administration, they appear to reflect the concerns and interests of students and practitioners of public affairs, and they facilitate discussion of associated values identified in Chapter 2.

Three of the themes are the public service values *neutrality*, *efficiency*, and *accountability*; they have always been at the center of the role of the public service practitioner in a democratic society. They connect with many other values that deserve attention, and they help to structure our discussion of the relationships between public service professionals, elected leaders, and the public at large.

The fourth theme in the book, *public service*, is about the personal commitment many public professionals experience, including the public service value of *integrity* and a desire to "make a difference" in society. *Public interest* is the fifth theme, moving from individual commitment to professional participation in governance decisions. Taken together, these five ideas capture a continuum of role behaviors in public service, from neutral implementation of the decisions of elected leaders to active involvement in creating and shaping policies and programs.

The context of professional work in public affairs is an important element in *Public Service Values*. The historical development of the culture surrounding public service organizations and the characteristics of the political and economic environment are more than influential in the work of public professionals. They are the context that creates and shapes that work; ultimately, culture and environment provide the criteria for evaluating what has been done. Though *Public Service Values* has been written in the context of American culture, the idea of studying administrative behavior in public service from the vantage point of values extends beyond national boundaries, appearing in many places.

People in any particular country will understandably find their specific interpretation of public service values especially interesting, but a notable part of the usefulness of study of public service values is the knowledge generated by comparing them across cultures. Comparative research and analysis can lead to broader understanding, functioning as a vehicle for examination of the relationship of public service values to culture and institutions in each country. To the extent this examination contributes to improvement in provision of public services, it is well worth the investment in time and attention. Comparative examination is not an explicit focus of *Public Service Values*, but the author will be pleased if the book serves as a platform for discussion of cross-national differences.

Public Service Values is designed as a supplemental text for graduate and undergraduate courses in public affairs. It should be useful in any course in which discussion of public service values will enrich the learning experience and offer a guide to professional practice. Students and instructors can discuss how they would apply public service values in different situations, what the trade-offs between values might be, and whether values might drive the choices made or serve as a way to understand actions after the fact. If the book is successful, it will make readers more aware of the importance of values in professional life, and it is the author's hope that it will contribute to a more conscious and reflective public practice.

I want to thank M.E. Sharpe and especially Executive Editor Harry Briggs, who has worked with me patiently through several book projects. Thanks also go to my colleagues in the Hauptmann School of Public Affairs at Park University; the values of the School played a significant part in the inspiration for this book. I am grateful to Mary R. Hamilton from the University of Nebraska at Omaha, and former executive director of the American Society for Public Administration, for writing the wonderful Foreword.

PUBLIC
SERVICE
VALUES

1

The Public Professional and Public Service Values

THE IMPORTANCE OF VALUES IN THE PUBLIC SECTOR

People often have something to say about values. We may read or hear phrases such as "That goes against her values" or "We support the values of the organization," but many times the values themselves are not named or described. If we know something about the people and the circumstances, we may have a general feeling about what values are implied. The concept remains vague, though—an appeal to imagine what values are at stake. For example, we might think, "She seems to care about protecting endangered species" or "That organization appears to be committed to delivering public services efficiently." Since the values in question have not been specifically identified, we may or may not accurately understand the perspectives and actions of the people involved.

Values have always been part of practice and research in public administration. From the beginnings of the modern era of American public administration in the late nineteenth century, values such as political neutrality, accountability, efficiency, honesty, integrity, and serving the public interest have been important. They continue to be important today, though people may think about them somewhat differently because of changes that have taken place in society.

A century and more ago, people who wrote about public administration favored a clearer separation between the politics of making laws and policies and the administrative work of managing public agencies. They were worried about political influence in basic functions such as hiring and promoting public employees, granting contracts for public projects, and deciding how public services would be delivered. To make public service more professional, reformers wanted partisan politics to be separated from the daily work of federal and state agencies and city and county departments. In this environment, we would expect a value such as *political neutrality* to be especially important. Neutrality suggests that career public professionals should do their work without regard to the demands or preferences of elected officials who might want them to hire a friend or relative, promote a certain policy orientation, give an attractive contract to a business the officials are associated with, or provide good services to people they favor while slighting others.

Neutrality is still important today, but the relationship between politics and administration, always complicated, can be even more difficult to sort out in the twenty-first century. We are no longer so interested in a clear separation of the two spheres, but we nevertheless recognize real and important differences between what political leaders do and what public professionals do. Here is another example of how perspectives on values can change with time. In the late 1960s and into the 1970s, a school of thought called *New Public Administration* emphasized *social equity* as a value. Social equity is about fairness and justice for everyone who interacts with government. (New Public Administration is not to be confused with the *New Public Management* of the 1990s. Also, social equity is not about economic equality, which is a very different concept.)

Discussion of social equity was a response to the social change occurring then; during the 1960s and into the 1970s Americans recognized the seriousness of problems in areas such as racial discrimination, voting rights, clean air and water, protection of wild and sensitive lands and wildlife, women's rights and roles in society, and extensive poverty in both urban and rural areas. Large-scale social movements formed and major federal laws and programs were created to deal with these issues. In public administration, social equity was initially given more attention by academicians than by public professionals, but it continues to be important today and has become a familiar value in teaching, research, and administrative practice. Advocates of New Public Administration assumed that the governments of advanced democracies, with their pluralistic, competitive politics, favor powerful, organized special interests as opposed to minorities who are without significant political and economic resources (Frederickson 1980, 7). Operating within existing laws and policies, public administrators could refocus governmental "responsiveness to the needs of citizens rather than the needs of public organizations" (6).

Since the 1980s, the public sector in many developed countries has experienced a significant shift in values, as ideas drawn from the private, market sector have been applied to government. In the United States in the 1980s, President Ronald Reagan and his administration moved away from the idea of government as a way of solving collective problems to characterizing government itself as the problem. They thought this situation could be dealt with by shrinking the public sector (though not the defense establishment) and allowing the states to take responsibility for some public services offered by the national government. The values held by the Reagan administration included self-government and individual freedom, in contrast to what they regarded as big-government liberalism and individual dependence on government.

In the 1990s, this shift toward favoring values of the private sector over those of the public sector moved into the specifics of administering public agencies. The idea of *reinventing government* (Osborne and Gaebler 1993) would have government run more like a private-sector business, emphasizing values and techniques such as entrepreneurship, innovativeness, profitability, performance measurement, and customer service. Importing these values into the public sector has inspired new ways of thinking about old problems, though values that work well in the private sector have not always fit comfortably into the legal, political, and operational context of the public sector (Box 1999).

The idea of running government like a business has been of more than academic interest, having significant effects on the daily operation of public agencies and the perspectives of public professionals. At the level of the structure of the public sector, today the idea that many services can and should be contracted out to nonprofit and private organizations is commonplace, and in some countries major public services have been privatized by being sold to private firms. At the level of daily organizational management, economic efficiency has become especially important, sometimes eclipsing values such as fairness and equity, social justice, constitutionalism and law, and citizen involvement in governance.

New Public Management (NPM) is a term commonly used to identify the application of private sector values to the public sector. It implies a connection with private sector management and distinguishes it from "administration," which we associate with the public sector. It can be thought of as a reaction to the growth of the public sector in the period following World War II. As government met the challenges of a rapidly growing population, expanding urban areas, and an increasingly global economy, it grew larger and more intrusive in the daily lives of citizens and business people. Not surprisingly, this produced a political reaction that continues today, with demands to shrink government and make it less costly. However, citizens who complain about the cost of government generally do not want fewer services and benefits—at least not for themselves—and business leaders who want less regulation of the private sector may also want good schools and infrastructure, protection from the trade practices of other nations, and subsidies for their businesses.

In response to problems with the application of private sector ideas to the public sector, a focus on the value of public sector action has been emerging in the past several years (Benington and Moore 2011; Bozeman 2007; Moore 1995). In public administration, there is increasing interest in a complex of ideas and values that includes collaboration between government, nonprofit and private organizations, and citizens (Box et al. 2001; Denhardt and Denhardt 2011). This shared system of decision making and service delivery can be called a *governance network* (Koliba, Meek, and

Zia 2011) or *New Public Governance* (Osborne 2010), and it can explicitly involve identifying and pursuing public values (Bao et al. 2012). Koliba, Meek, and Zia (2011, 31–35) suggest that such a governance system brings together the formal hierarchy and accountability of "classical" public administration; the competition and compromise of the market model; the collaboration and cooperation characteristic of government partnerships with private firms, nonprofits, and citizens; and the coordination of the activities of those working within a network.

Identifying, discussing, negotiating, and acting on the values held by everyone in a governance network can be complicated and demanding. Only time will tell to what extent this view of governance replaces the market-based values of NPM and how common its core values become in administrative practice. Meanwhile, though, it supports the idea that values are today, as they have always been, important in government and the public service.

A FOCUS ON THE PUBLIC PROFESSIONAL

The focus of this book is on values and the daily work of career public professionals. It is not uncommon in books about public administration to find the roles of public professionals, political appointees, and elected leaders mixed together as if they were the same, but they are quite different. Public professionals, political appointees, and elected leaders are different in how they are chosen for their positions, to whom they are accountable, what laws and policies determine the work they do, and what expectations members of the public have for their work performance and ethical standards. Given these role differences, we can expect that people in these three types of public sector roles identify and prioritize values differently.

When categories are applied to a complex situation, there will often be gray areas and exceptions. Nevertheless, a set of working definitions can be used in our examination of public service values. *Elected leaders* are just that; citizens choose them through election. They are accountable to the electorate, they follow the federal or state constitution or state and local laws applicable to local government, and they are involved in creating new laws at their level of government. The public expects them to show at least some awareness of the preferences of the majority of the people who elected them. The public also prefers that elected leaders behave in an ethical manner, but people may not be especially surprised when it is revealed that their elected officials are instead involved in personal, political, or financial misbehavior.

Political appointees are chosen by an elected leader such as the president or governor because they have demonstrated loyalty to a particular party or ideology or because they have relevant experience or expertise. (At the local level, there are political appointees in some places, but many governmental units have structural systems that do not include this category of leadership.) Cabinet secretaries (Defense, Treasury, and so on at the national level; departments of health services, natural resources, corrections, and so on at the state level), White House staff, and several thousand people who are appointed by the president to serve in senior agency management are all political appointees. Some of them will serve beyond the term of the elected official who appointed them, but most will leave office at the same time that person leaves. Political appointees are accountable to the appointing elected official (though they may also consider themselves accountable to, for example, the public, a party, or a view of the public interest); their actions are constrained by constitutions, laws, policies, and public expectations; and they are expected to have some capability or expertise related to the organization they lead. As with elected officials, the public would prefer that political appointees behave in an ethical manner, but occasional misbehavior is not unexpected.

Career public professionals (we can also use terms such as *public-service practitioners*) are never chosen by election. Instead, most are chosen in formal hiring systems that assess education, experience, and possibly performance on written and oral examinations. They are selected based on qualifications rather than personal or party loyalty or ideology, and most will serve across the terms of elected officials. Public professionals are accountable to those who appoint them, to the elected leadership of their organizations, and to the public at large. The roles of public pro-

private-sector activities regulated by government can illustrate this point: safe food and drugs; the air transport system; defense, police, fire, and emergency services; water and sewer systems; the national parks and forests; and streets and highways. We can choose which private-sector goods and services to consume, but we cannot avoid paying for and receiving the benefits of public services.

Another key characteristic of the public sector is that its primary function is to provide services people have decided upon collectively. The primary public-sector function is not making a profit for owners or shareholders; it is supporting communities from the local to the national level by doing those things citizens expect of government in an advanced democratic society.

A third characteristic that differentiates the public sector from the private and nonprofit sectors is that its structures and functions are defined by national and state constitutions and administrative regulations and, at the local level, by state constitutions, laws, and home-rule charters. This may sound dry or trivial, but it is neither. Instead, these structures and functions shape the working environment of public professionals, the way decisions are made and implemented in government, and the impacts of governmental actions on the lives of individual citizens.

Finally, the public sector is different because we expect it to operate with transparency and accountability. These are key values of a democratic society. Without transparency, the people cannot make knowledgeable choices between candidates and policies; without accountability, the people do not know whether the choices they have made are being implemented.

This analysis leads to the conclusion that government matters, as do the values used to guide governmental action. Studying public service values should make it easier to use them in daily decision making and also to change how values are prioritized or defined so they better serve the ends we want to achieve.

A Specific Sort of Values

To this point, we have discussed values without defining what they are. The idea of values is broad and open-ended, so exact definitions are elusive. Even so, it will be helpful to adopt a definition or description that makes the subject somewhat clearer. Barry Bozeman (2007, 117), in the book *Public Values and Public Interest: Counterbalancing Economic Individualism*, suggests a definition of values that seems useful here as well:

> A value is a complex and broad-based assessment of an object or set of objects (where the objects may be concrete, psychological, socially constructed, or a combination of all three) characterized by both cognitive and emotive elements, arrived at after some deliberation, and, because a value is part of the individual's definition of self, it is not easily changed and it has the potential to elicit action.

This complicated definition contains, according to Bozeman (117), six assumptions:

1. Values express evaluative judgments.
2. Values have *both* cognitive and emotional aspects.
3. Values are relatively stable.
4. Values have the strong potential to affect behavior.
5. Values change (if at all) only after deliberation.
6. Values help define one's sense of oneself.

Following this definition, we find that values bring together emotion and rational thought, they are relatively stable over time, and they may well influence behavior. It is important to recognize that values are *subjective*—that is, they are not fixed, certain, and given to us to accept or reject. As we will find in Chapter 2, there are a number of values that many public professionals believe to be important. However, though some values are shared by large numbers of people in public service, the experiences that have led individuals to hold certain values, what they think the values mean, and how they apply them in daily professional life present a wide range of differences that make even shared values more complex than they may seem initially.

To put this another way, values are a human construction, not a phenomenon somehow imposed on people from an external source. Because values have been discussed for millennia and are a deeply ingrained part of human society, existing values provide guidance about the norms of the human community and they may make a particular person feel some pressure to adopt certain values to fit in with peers. Still, the responsibility for choosing, defining, and applying values is ours alone, as individuals.

This book has a more specific focus than the idea of public values generally; the focus is on values held by career public professionals which can be used to guide their work. *Public service values* are related to the institutional and legal structures of government and are relevant for people who answer, ultimately, to an elected governing body. There are also wider networks of governing relationships that include contractors, nonprofit organizations, community groups, and others. Some of these groups, organizations, and people may do work related to the public sector through funding, legal requirements, and a specific public purpose to be achieved. Examples are a company manufacturing aircraft for the U.S. Air Force, an engineering firm producing highway or street construction drawings for a state or local government, and a nonprofit organization providing mental health services by contract with a county government, in a program with federal government funding. Other groups, organizations, and people may function as centers of influence or decision making outside of government, though they are not directly involved in providing public services. Examples are neighborhood association members participating in a city planning process for their area and a nonprofit environmental organization providing input to a federal agency during discussion of proposals for managing wilderness areas.

The challenges of supervising contracted public services are well known; monitoring cost, quality, and reporting is more complicated for a public agency when the people delivering a service work for nongovernmental organizations. The employees of those organizations are not subject to the constraints and expectations experienced by employees in public agencies, nor do they necessarily share the values common in the public sector. Nevertheless, the contracted programs carry with them requirements applicable to the public sector, so public professionals are responsible for ensuring appropriate performance.

When people outside of government participate in a policy-making process that involves multiple centers of influence, the potential for conflicting views is significant. If everyone interested in a policy issue shared the same values, purposes, and desired ends, there would be little need for a process allowing exchange of views, examination of alternative solutions, and agreement on compromise solutions. Given that differences are likely in these settings, facilitation skills and an openness to multiple perspectives are useful for public professionals. For our examination of public service values, the point is to be aware that people inside and outside government may have different views of values and purposes, in part because of the unique legal and institutional context of the public sector.

We need to take care in generalizing about values in the public sector, for two reasons. First, the public sector is complex and there are multiple levels and types of governments: the state and national governments, regional governments, cities, counties, and special districts for schools, air quality, utilities, and so on. In total, there are more than 89,000 units of government in the United States, so we can assume that emphasis on certain values varies by geographic area, the size and purposes of a governmental jurisdiction, and the characteristics of the population served.

Second, though there are values of interest to most people who work in government, many values that make a real difference in the work of public professionals are occupationally specific. This is a point rarely addressed in discussions of public sector values, but those of us who teach courses in which values are part of the dialogue discover that public professionals who have only slight familiarity with values such as neutrality or the public interest (which are applicable across the public sector) are deeply committed to values shared by others who do similar work. Examples include the importance of strong families and safe children for a case worker in children's protective services, the safety of the nation for a military officer, emergency preparedness for a staff person in a state emergency management agency, and economic and ecological sustainability for a planner in a city planning agency.

Given some background information, any of us could develop an appreciation for the values that inspire these people to do their best every day, but without someone calling our attention to these values we would probably have given them little thought. It would be quite a project to identify a wide range of occupationally specific values, but a number of values common across the public sector are discussed thoroughly in the literature of the field. For practical if not principled reasons, we will focus on values of interest to the entire public sector, keeping in mind that there are also other values people care about and use in their daily work.

The specific sort of values studied here, public service values, can be of real importance in the lives of public professionals and citizens. As Bozeman notes, values have the capacity to shape behavior, and the actions taken by public administrators can affect the lives of many people and the condition of the physical environment. Though values in the public sector may seem largely of interest to researchers and teachers, research on values draws evidence from practice, researchers are often the same people who teach students in public administration, and public service values have become central to the process of accrediting master's programs in public administration, public policy, and public affairs. This circular relationship, in which practice influences theory and theory influences practice, reinforces the idea that discussion of public service values is worthwhile.

DEVELOPMENT OF THE CONTEXT OF PUBLIC SERVICE

Politics and economics in society can have significant and lasting effects on what it is like to work in public service. Sometimes elected leaders think of the public sector as a useful tool for addressing collective problems and sometimes they attack government as big and wasteful and public professionals as unresponsive and privileged. During difficult economic periods, cutbacks in the public sector make it challenging to maintain adequate staffing and desired levels of service delivery. Along with these trends come changes in public programs, public employee job stability and compensation, and expectations for accountability to elected leaders.

Because the societal context can be so important in shaping conditions in the public sector, it will be useful to briefly recount how it developed. Today, we seem to be experiencing an increasing rate of change, a fading sense of collective responsibility and capacity to choose effective solutions to problems, reduction of values to raw economic calculation, and a public deeply skeptical about government.

These characteristics of society have not developed randomly, but come from the dynamic interaction between the culture, which is shaped by the nation's origin and history, and today's national and global conditions. The relationship of the American public to government is influenced by the historical experience of occupying a new continent and separating from colonial rule. This occurred during the *Age of Enlightenment* in the seventeenth and eighteenth centuries, a time when people were beginning to think independently about the nature of society rather than accepting without question the views of religious leaders and monarchs.

In what later became the United States, the *Declaration of Independence* emphasized individual liberty as a value. The *U.S. Constitution* took effect more than a decade later (in 1789), organizing a new government based on a desire for a more cohesive nation that would promote stability, protection of property, and economic prosperity. The new government was created in a secretive process and over the objections of many leaders and citizens in the states, it was based on a view of human nature as often self-interested, and, at the national level, it allowed the people relatively little opportunity to participate in choosing leaders or policies. The resulting design separated the powers of the national government between branches to prevent domination by any one person or group, and it divided responsibility for governing between the states and the new national government (Allen, Lloyd, and Lloyd 1985; Quinn 1993). The public debates over the new constitution often reflected conflict grounded in economic issues between ordinary citizens and the wealthy and powerful (Wood 1969).

These elements—a nation created from the experience of fleeing the power of church and state, and a government structure that divides powers at the national level and creates a national-state system—did not produce the sort of centralized, institutionalized administration found in some other countries. They also did not immediately create an administrative apparatus suited to running the new government. Instead, public administration in the United States was built up slowly, through many decades of trial and error, sorting through different approaches to issues such as political influence in personnel and administrative functions and, in local government, political versus professional administrative leadership. What we think of today as the role of the career public professional is the result of the work of generations of people who believed in the application of technical knowledge and rational decision making (values in themselves) to governmental actions and delivery of public services.

This historical development took place in a society with a *mixed economy*, a situation in which most economic enterprises are privately owned, but government regulates economic activity to stabilize economic conditions and to minimize the negative effects of the market on people and the physical environment. Mixed economies can have a governmental sector that is a large part of the economy or one that is a relatively small part of the economy. Despite the complaints of Americans who think the public sector is too large and expensive, in the United States government at all levels is relatively limited in scope and economic impact in relation to governments in many other developed nations.

Public administration in this sort of mixed economy is a balancing act, finding trade-offs among economic interests, the interests of individuals and groups, and the health of the air, water, climate, and environmentally sensitive lands and wildlife. In part because of the values present in society when the nation was created and the way in which public administration developed, the professional public service generally has a weak position in American society compared to its status in many other developed countries (Stillman 1991). People working for government often cannot impose solutions in isolation, but must instead work with others in a facilitative role to explore alternatives and find solutions that are acceptable to a number of groups and individuals.

Though most people in public service share a commitment to fair and impartial action guided by accumulated knowledge and expertise, many citizens think of those who work in government as power-hungry people who waste tax dollars. This is the legacy of a cultural and institutional history in which citizens have wanted government to deal with public problems but at the same time to remain weak and limited. This contradiction between effective collective action and individual liberty, between "public purpose" and "private interest" (Schlesinger 1986, 27), is at the heart of the challenge of being a public professional in America.

FIVE VALUE THEMES IN PUBLIC SERVICE

There are many ways an examination of public service values could be organized, and there are multiple sources of professional values. Here are two interesting approaches to organizing a discussion of values that may be used as examples. Probably the most comprehensive treatment of the subject is Montgomery Van Wart's book *Changing Public Sector Values*, published in 1998. Van Wart uses a five-part framework consisting of individual values, professional values, organizational values, legal values, and public interest values. This framework allows him to explore a wide range of related ideas and issues, such as the characteristics of professions, leadership types, subordination of public administration to the law and the courts, efficient and effective use of resources, and types of control of administrative action.

In a book chapter published in 1989, Charles Goodsell also offered a five-part characterization of what he called "value orientations." His five categories (the "Five Ms") are a *means* orientation, in which the administrator is "the passive tool of higher authority" (576); a *morality* orientation, including values such as "equality, justice, honesty, fairness, and the protection of individual rights" (577); a *multitude* orientation, in which "the administrator responds neither to elected officials nor to a higher authority, but to the citizens themselves" (577); a *market* orientation, in which agencies use techniques such as user fees and contracting services; and a *mission* orientation, in which administrators are important actors in shaping and implementing the mission of their agencies, along with legislators, the courts, and others.

Goodsell's five-part system parallels longstanding concepts in public administration and developments that have occurred in recent decades. The means orientation identifies the traditional expectation that public employees will maintain an attitude of political neutrality in their work, favoring no particular party or person. The morality orientation is about administrative ethics, examination of the moral and ethical foundations of administrative action. *Citizen involvement*—working with citizens to provide information, facilitating discussion of policy options, and helping people participate in the policy-making process— is an important model of administrative action. As Goodsell notes in describing the multitude orientation, this was part of the New Public Administration school of thought in the 1960s and 1970s.

The economic assumptions underlying NPM are found in Goodsell's market orientation, though NPM as an identifiable school of thought developed later on in the United States. In contrast to the means orientation, in which administrators simply carry out directives from political leaders and superiors, the mission orientation regards public professionals as partners in the process of governing. This view corresponds to the discussion of *administrative legitimacy* that became prominent in the 1980s in an effort to counter the weak position of public administration in the American system of government. This school of thought argued that public administration should be recognized as a significant and valid part of the constitutional order (Wamsley et al. 1987).

As with Van Wart's five-part framework, Goodsell's five value orientations offer opportunities to discuss a range of values, schools of thought, and patterns of development in public administration theory and practice. In addition to frameworks such as these, public service values can be found in topical areas such as administrative ethics, codes of ethics of professional associations, and the literature of democracy and citizen involvement in governance. They can also be found in the code of ethics of the American Society for Public Administration (ASPA) and the accreditation standards of the Network of Schools of Public Policy, Affairs, and Administration (NASPAA).

Each of these sources of public service values is discussed in Chapter 2, but this is a good time to outline the public service values framework of the book. Because so many different values have been used in the public sector and so many sources are available, identifying which values to discuss or deciding how to organize them is not easy. Mark Rutgers (2008) has suggested that people who write about public service values should make an effort to explain why they have chosen particular values and organized them in a certain way. *Public Service Values* is not a scholarly exercise in finding and describing as many public service values as possible and organizing them into a logical system that can compete for acceptance with other similar systems. Instead, the purpose here is to offer a guide to values that can be useful in daily practice. Accordingly, the values discussed are found often in the published literature of public administration practice and theory and have strong connections with the history of the field and the development of major schools of thought.

Values can change over time, in content and in emphasis, depending on conditions in society. The reader may have noticed that in books and articles on public administration it is not unusual for a particular approach to theory and practice to be called "new." The claim is often made that a supposedly new idea is very different from "old" ("traditional" or "classical") public administration. Such claims usually have some truth in them, along with a tendency to give the misleading impression that public professionals in past decades did not do the things that people in public service do now or will do in the future.

Two examples are efficiency and citizen involvement. First, competent government managers have always been interested in maximizing service quality and quantity for a given amount of available resources. However, someone learning about NPM might think that public professionals have until now ignored economic efficiency, which is only recently becoming important in the public sector. Second, it has been true for decades that many public professionals engage in dialogue with citizens about public policies and service delivery. The trend toward organized citizen involvement was fully underway in the 1970s, but someone reading today about governance networks might think that past generations of public professionals have huddled in their offices, avoiding contact with the outside world and doing their work in ignorance of public needs and preferences.

The point is that not everything is "new": many of the challenges and techniques common in public service today also existed in the past. There can be changes in emphasis, though, and in important ways today's society is significantly different from that experienced by public professionals in the past, given the effects of globalization, technology, market-like thought, and other factors. Kenneth Kernaghan (2003, 717) has drawn a distinction between long-term "core" values and other values that seem to come and go: "In determining the core values, it is necessary to assess the staying power of new professional values, such as innovation and entrepreneurship, which are closely linked to the NPM movement. Twenty years ago, these values would not have been ranked as core public-service values."

Another key point in organizing a discussion of public service values is that there are so many that it helps to group them into types, as illustrated by the Van Wart and Goodsell examples above. To do this, we can use "nodal values," which Jørgensen and Bozeman (2007, 370) identify as appearing "to occupy a central position in a network of values"; this provides a framework for discussing a wide range of related values.

The organizing framework in *Public Service Values* consists of five themes. The first three themes, associated with Chapters 3, 4, and 5, focus on values that define the professional role: *neutrality*, *efficiency*, and *accountability*. The fourth theme, addressed in Chapter 6, is *public service*, which is about the value commitments of individual public professionals. The fifth theme, discussed in Chapter 7, is *public interest*. This is about values that professionals apply to action on public programs and policies. As noted in the Preface, these five themes align with central issues discussed in the research literature of public administration, they appear to reflect the concerns and interests of students and practitioners of public affairs, and they facilitate discussion of associated values identified in Chapter 2.

In Chapter 2 we explore various models and sources of public service values, and then in turn each theme is examined in Chapters 3 through 7. Chapter 8 draws the themes together with final thoughts about values and public service. I hope the reader finds *Public Service Values* interesting in itself and useful in professional practice.

2

Public Service Values Today

SOURCES OF PUBLIC SERVICE VALUES

In part, public service values originate in the daily work of service delivery, when public professionals reflect on the ideas, judgments, and emotions underlying their decisions and actions. Values also come from the environment of public administration, as elected leaders and citizens think about the relationship of the public sector to society and what they want it to achieve. We may become especially aware of values when they appear in the publications of professional organizations and in articles and books written by researchers in the field.

Discussion of public service values can be found in many places. Though we should make an effort to find as many important public service values as we can, this does not require an exhaustive review of articles, books, websites, and so on. Instead, we can identify several key sources of public service values and search for commonalities, values that practitioners and academicians in public affairs think are especially useful.

The first source to be discussed is research that inventories values or surveys public professionals to discover what is important to them. This material brings us close to knowing which values influence daily practice and the conduct of public organizations. There are five more source categories discussed in this chapter. Immediately following values identified in research studies, we turn to the sort of value typologies described in Chapter 1 with the work of Montgomery Van Wart and Charles Goodsell, and then examine administrative ethics, democracy, codes of ethics, and the accreditation standards of the Network of Schools of Public Policy, Affairs, and Administration.

STUDIES OF PUBLIC SERVICE VALUES

Drawing from books and articles on ethics and values, Zeger Van der Wal and Leo Huberts (2008) identified a set of values to use in a large survey of Dutch managers in public and private organizations. They found clear differences and also considerable agreement between people in the two sectors; the managers' rank ordering of the importance of values is especially interesting.

Respondents in both sectors found nine values to be "relatively important": accountability, dedication, effectiveness, expertise, honesty, incorruptibility, lawfulness, reliability, and transparency (273). Public-sector managers emphasized these values: incorruptibility, accountability, honesty, lawfulness, reliability, effectiveness, expertise, and transparency (274). The top values for private-sector managers were reliability, honesty, expertise, incorruptibility, effectiveness, accountability, efficiency, profitability, lawfulness, transparency, innovativeness, and dedication (275).

Though some values overlapped the two sectors, there were also differences that fit classic sectoral characterizations. As Van der Wal and Huberts put it, "at the core of government and business differences seem to be impartiality and incorruptibility (public), and profitability and innovativeness (private), although it should be noted that incorruptibility received high rates in companies as well" (276).

Torben Beck Jørgensen and Barry Bozeman (2007) examined public administration periodicals from the United States, United Kingdom, and Scandinavian countries published between 1990 and 2003, identifying values in seven categories. These categories included, for example, the relationship between public administrators and their environment, the relationship between public administrators and politicians, and the behavior of public-sector employees. This research dealt only with values discussed in the public sector and the values are not rank ordered, but there are parallels with the values ranked highly by public managers in the Van der Wal and Huberts study. Accountability, honesty, lawfulness/

rule of law, reliability, effectiveness, and expertise/professionalism appear in both studies. In addition, Jørgensen and Bozeman's survey of values in the research literature found additional values worth considering, such as public interest, human dignity, democracy, citizen involvement, justice, and friendliness.

In a survey and interviews with fifty-two state and local public professionals in the Midwest, Anthony Molina and Cassandra McKeown (2012) began with twenty values that had been used earlier by Van der Wal and Huberts. They added five values adapted from the *Code of Ethics* of the American Society for Public Administration (ASPA) and five taken from an article written by Kenneth Kernaghan (2003). The people who participated in the survey included city managers, finance officers, public school superintendents, law enforcement administrators, and others in local government. State government participants were from health and human services, education, transportation, and other service areas.

One of the tasks Molina and McKeown gave respondents was to name the five values of the list of thirty that were most important in their work. Figure 2.1 shows the results, with the numbers on the right side of the bars showing how many times each value was rated in the top five. Honesty was chosen most often as an important value, followed by integrity, accountability, and dedication, then reliability and expertise. (Definitions for the values in the study are given in Appendix A.) These values describe traditional characteristics of the role played by public professionals in a democratic society, rather than policy preferences, outcome and performance measures, or interactions with others in a network.

Values we often connect with the market paradigm of New Public Management (NPM) (sometimes called "running government like a business"), such as efficiency, innovativeness, and profitability, were not chosen as frequently. The same is true of values we would associate with intersectoral (network) and participatory governance, such as participativeness (involving citizens in administrative decision making), representativeness (acting according to citizens' values), and pluralism (accommodating a diverse citizenry).

It should be noted that participants rated twenty-six of the thirty values as "usually important" in a separate set of questions in which the four choices were unimportant, sometimes important,

Figure 2.1 **Administrators' Ranking of Most Important Values**

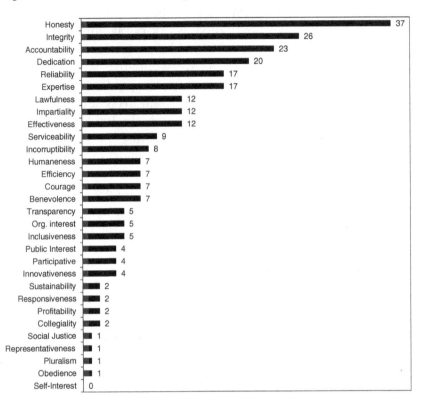

Source: Molina and McKeown (2012, 385).

usually important, or always important (Molina and McKeown 2012, 379). Four values were at the bottom of this ranking, with average scores in the "sometimes important" range: participative, sustainability, self-interest, and, in the last position, profitability.

This is just a single small study. Research involving different professional specializations, level of government, level of employees in a hierarchy, geographic areas, or numbers of participants could produce quite different results. Even so, studies such as these three and others provide a set of public service values to work with in more detail. They tell us there are values that are recognized as important in public service and that people have identified, discussed, and conducted research about them.

An interesting cross-national study of public service values was conducted by Lijing Yang and Zeger Van der Wal, who administered a survey followed by interviews of public affairs students (many of whom were practicing public professionals) in China and the Netherlands. Using a set of twenty-five values, the researchers asked respondents to identify ideal public service values they think important and actual values that make a difference in their daily work. Of the ideal values, "six of the top ten values for both groups were shared: lawfulness, expertise, people-oriented, impartiality, incorruptibility, and responsibility" (Yang and Van der Wal 2014, 196).

Given the contrasting cultures, some differences are to be expected; they appeared with values such as transparency, ranked first by the Dutch respondents and fifteenth by the Chinese. Reliability was ranked third by the Dutch and twenty-second in China (197). However, values that could be considered "Confucian," such as "righteousness, incorruptibility, and honesty appeared among the top ten ideal type values for the Netherlands but not in the top ten for China" (197). At the same time, "Chinese civil servants prioritized professional and law-based values such as efficiency, effectiveness, equality, and accountability, whereas some of these were (relatively) less important in the Netherlands" (197).

In comparison to the ranking of ideal values, Yang and Van der Wal found greater value differences between the Chinese and Dutch respondents in values actually important in daily work life. There were four highly ranked actual values common to the two groups: lawfulness, efficiency, effectiveness, and expertise. However, the most important value was different in China and the Netherlands, with obedience chosen in China and effectiveness in the Netherlands (197). The authors found that actual values important to the Chinese respondents are "quite Confucian" and those important to the Dutch are "more Western" (197). Though obedience, loyalty, and diligence were not in the top ten ideal values chosen by the Chinese, they were in their top ten of actual values in use (197).

Differences between the two sets of respondents also appeared in the values identified as least important. For the Chinese, the least important values were courage, propriety, efficiency, transparency, and innovativeness. The least important values for the Dutch were courage, obedience, innovativeness, responsiveness, and social justice (197). It is interesting that despite the discussion of NPM in China, efficiency and innovativeness were among the least important values for the Chinese respondents.

Another part of the survey, which asked questions about issues of "professional morality," also revealed differences and similarities between the Chinese and Dutch participants. The Chinese "showed more loyalty toward their superiors than the Dutch respondents" and "considered personal relationships to be more crucial for their career development." However, both sets of respondents "equally valued personal morals as more important than rules or regulations" (200).

The commonalities and differences found in this study show the complexity of the interaction of culture and values globally. Yang and Van der Wal found that "Chinese respondents increasingly appreciate the Western professional civil service ethos, but their actual value preferences show more traditional differences." Also, "a considerable number of Confucian values were highly ranked by Dutch respondents, and they too value self-cultivation and personal morality as elements in their professional ethos" (202). Though the Dutch and Chinese cultures are very different and this study found some interesting differences in public service values, the similarities across cultures were notable as well.

Value Typologies

In the section discussing "five values themes in public service" in Chapter 1, two examples are given of ways to organize and describe public service values. One is Montgomery Van Wart's (1998) framework of individual values, professional values, organizational values, legal values, and public interest values. The other is Charles Goodsell's (1989) "value orientations" (the "Five M's"): a means orientation, a morality orientation, a multitude orientation, a market orientation, and a mission orientation.

Here are two more value typologies that offer interesting perspectives. Kenneth Kernaghan (2003, 712) suggests that public service values could be organized in four categories, as shown in Table 2.1.

Table 2.1

Kernaghan's Categories of Public Service Values

Ethical	Democratic	Professional	People
Integrity	Rule of law	Effectiveness	Caring
Fairness	Neutrality	Efficiency	Fairness
Accountability	Accountability	Service	Tolerance
Loyalty	Loyalty	Leadership	Decency
Excellence	Openness	Excellence	Compassion
Respect	Responsiveness	Innovation	Courage
Honesty	Representativeness	Quality	Benevolence
Probity	Legality	Creativity	Humanity

This value set is not unlike the one used by Molina and McKeown, though there are some additional entries, notably those values in the category "People." Humaneness, benevolence, and social justice appear in the Molina and McKeown list; Kernaghan's list adds caring, fairness, tolerance, decency, and compassion. Taken together, the two lists show considerable attention to social conditions and humane administrative behavior. Kernaghan's four categories seem to capture especially important dimensions of public sector practice: acting ethically, paying attention to the role of the public service practitioner in a democratic society, serving in a professional manner, and caring about the effects of administrative action on the public.

Gene Brewer, Sally Coleman Selden, and Rex Facer (2000) created a unique characterization of the service motivations of public professionals. They described four role categories for these motivations: *Samaritans, communitarians, patriots, and humanitarians.* The authors asked sixty-nine local, state, and federal employees in several states to rate how strongly they agreed with several statements related to public service motivation. The study participants worked in "administration (accounting, budgeting, personnel, etc.), agriculture, education, finance, health care, human services, law enforcement, recreation, sanitation, transportation, and the military" (256). With interview results in hand, the researchers used a statistical technique to identify the four categories of values and they gave them names that capture the reader's attention. Here are descriptions of each category, in the words of the authors, beginning with Samaritans.

[Samaritans] . . . are strongly motivated to help other people. They see themselves as guardians of the underprivileged and are moved emotionally when they observe people in distress. (258–259)

[Communitarians are] . . . motivated and stirred by sentiments of civic duty and public service. . . . Communitarians believe there is a unique connection between public servants and citizens. According to this group, public service is "one of the highest forms of citizenship"— an avenue by which a person can serve his or her community and country. (259)

Patriots act for causes much bigger than themselves . . . , protecting, advocating, and working for the good of the public. As Buchanan (1975, 425–427) suggested, this group has a unique sense of loyalty to duty; they put "duty before self. . . ." Not only is duty more important than self, but individuals in this group "would risk personal loss to help someone else. . . ." These individuals see themselves as guardians of the people, placing their obligation and responsibility to the public ahead of their loyalty to superiors and their own needs. (259–260)

Humanitarians are motivated by a strong sense of social justice and public service. . . . Like Samaritans, this group values many public causes and programs and views government as a vehicle for making society fair. . . . While humanitarians are touched by the plight of the underprivileged, their welfare concerns are more societal than Samaritans. . . . They believe that if any group is excluded from society's prosperity, the entire society is worse off. (260)

These four public service motivation types contain values that connect with the other lists and typologies we have discussed. Samaritans are interested in values found in Kernaghan's "People" column, such as caring, compassion, benevolence, and humanity. Communitarians value the public interest (identified by Molina and McKeown), patriots value loyalty and duty, and humanitarians focus on social justice and fairness.

In an article asserting the importance of values in public affairs degree programs, Rebekkah Stuteville and Laurie DiPadova-Stocks (2011) developed a typology of values drawn from the work of several authors, including some of those discussed above. In highlighting the commonalities in these studies, they wrote that "the shared values include integrity, representativeness, effectiveness, efficiency, and due process of law, as well as many others" (594). Given their examination of studies on public service values, Stuteville and DiPadova-Stocks concluded that "there appears to be at least implicit agreement on the core values in the discipline of public administration and the field of public service" (594). So, whether it is because the people conducting research on public service values are discussing them with one another or because there are indeed key values in use in public organizations, there is a measure of agreement on what those values are.

VALUES AND ADMINISTRATIVE ETHICS

When people think about ethics in the public sector, often what comes to mind is the personal misbehavior of elected leaders, the sort of scandals that are featured in the 24/7 media cycle and that give comedians material for jokes on television. In public administration, though, ethics is only partially about "right and wrong," and only rarely is it about personal misbehavior. Though taking care to avoid conflict of interest, misuse of government resources, and behavior that damages the reputation of one's organization are important, administrative ethics focuses mostly on the grounds for deciding what to do and how to do it.

In a complex democratic society, people who work in the public sector balance competing demands and may function to facilitate decision making among groups and individuals rather than acting on their own. This broad societal framework shapes the administrative role, which consists of the expectations held by organizational coworkers and superiors, peers in other organizations, elected leaders, and citizens for how public service practitioners carry out their responsibilities. With that understanding of the administrative role in mind, any of several sources of ethical guidance may be used in choosing a course of action.

Ethics in public administration is a large field of writing, research, and practice, too large to present here beyond sketching its relevance for public service values. James Svara's (2015) three-part characterization of philosophical approaches to ethics in the public and nonprofit sectors summarizes important ethical values in a way that can be of help. The three approaches are *virtue*, *principle*, and *consequences*; in the language of ethics, principle is "deontological" and consequential ethics are "teleological."

Virtue ethics are intuitive: "one grasps in a holistic way what a good person would do in a given situation," and "the virtuous person manifests and acts on the characteristics that mark one as a person of character and integrity" (Svara 2015, 61). Michael Josephson (2006) describes "six pillars of character," with related values. The pillars (shown in italics) and related values are as follows:

- *Trustworthiness*, with honesty, integrity, reliability (promise keeping), and loyalty;
- *Respect*, with civility, courtesy, and decency;
- *Responsibility*, with accountability, pursuit of excellence, and self-restraint;
- *Fairness*, with consistency, equality, openness, due process, impartiality, and equity;
- *Caring*, with causing no more harm than necessary, and benevolence; and
- *Citizenship*, with civic virtues and duties.

Clearly, there are overlaps here with the findings in studies of public service values and in value typologies. Svara points out that virtue ethics have advantages and disadvantages; advantages include "easy accessibility to ethical standards" (63) and the emphasis on goodness, which everyone can support. Disadvantages include the problem of putting virtues into action and the problem of balancing virtues against accountability and the directives of superiors and elected leaders.

Administrative ethics based on principle uses predetermined concepts to guide ethical choice. There are a number of potential sources for ethical principles, including laws, the Constitution, and generally agreed-upon principles such as truth telling and justice (Svara 2015, 66–69). Drawing from the work of David Rosenbloom, Svara (68–69) notes constitutional protections for substantive rights such as freedom of speech, due process, and equal protection, along with principles from constitutional amendments, such as protection from unreasonable search and seizure. Difficulties with the principled approach to ethics include the problem of conflicting principles, dealing with exceptions, and situations for which no principles are available. Advantages include external guidance for decision making and guidance about how one should act (69–72).

Finally, the consequences approach to ethics judges whether an action is ethical by the nature of the outcome. One way to evaluate the outcome is by using the *utilitarian* measure, which holds that actions that produce the greatest good for the greatest number are the most ethical. The idea of considering outcomes instead of principles has the advantage of tailoring ethical decision making to the situation at hand, rather than using an abstract concept that may or may not be especially helpful. However, choosing values to measure the desirability of outcomes can be difficult (how do we know what is good?), and we cannot know with certainty what will happen in the future (Svara 2015, 74–75).

Concepts from the virtue, principle, and consequences approaches can be used together, offering the benefits of each and helping to avoid the disadvantages. For our exploration of values, administrative ethics yields interesting ideas that we can include in a collection of public service values. Though many values that emerge from the study of ethics are the same as those found in research on public service values, the philosophical framework of the field of ethics goes beyond a listing, offering historical, explanatory, and normative perspectives on specific value concepts.

DEMOCRACY AS A SOURCE OF VALUES

The idea of democracy is central to American culture and government. Related values include democratic participation, giving citizens opportunities to contribute to the creation and implementation of public policies and programs, openness and transparency in governance, and representativeness, in which public professionals act in ways that reflect the values held by citizens. In today's large and complex urban society, it can be difficult for individual citizens to be meaningfully involved in the public sector. Not all government agencies and functions are well suited to do their work in a way we might think of as democratic, nor is it always easy, or even appropriate, to make them open and available to public involvement in creating and implementing public policies. Nevertheless, if the values of participativeness, openness, transparency, and representativeness are to be meaningful in the public sector, it is important to think about ways that citizens can contribute to governance.

In the classic view of public administration, elected leaders sense what citizens want done, they pass laws accordingly, and career public employees carry them out. This is the expected cycle of policy making and implementation in a *representative democracy*. In the eighteenth century, the national government in the United States was designed to allow citizens to vote on their leaders periodically, but they were not expected to participate more directly in governing. Most people of the time were poorly educated, leaders regarded them as incapable of making sound decisions on matters of public importance, and the national capital was a long, difficult journey away for much of the population.

State government was—and is—somewhat more accessible to citizens, but the same representative cycle of policy making and implementation is found here. At both the national and state levels today, this classic pattern has been modified by systems intended to gather the public's ideas about planned legislation and regulations, and by the technology that makes so much of government immediately visible and accessible. Nevertheless, the underlying model remains that of representative democracy.

Unlike the national and state governments, which are modeled on a *separation of powers* structure with three branches, legislative, executive, and judicial, local governments use a variety of structures. Though in many places local leaders largely exclude citizens from participating in governance beyond the act of voting or commenting on pending decisions, in other places residents join neighborhood organizations that work with city and county governments and special districts such as schools, volunteer to serve on governmental committees dealing with public issues, and organize their neighbors to influence public decision making. This is *direct democracy*, in which citizens can be said to "self-govern."

The idea of citizen involvement in local governance is an old one. In the nineteenth century, opportunities increased for ordinary citizens to become involved in community politics. During the Progressive Era in the early twentieth century, citizens gathered in neighborhood and community organizations to discuss the public issues of the day. In the 1960s, citizen participation became especially visible because the national government funded local activities related to planning and social services. In the next decades, citizen involvement programs grew in states, counties, and cities nationwide, changing the way local issues were addressed (Box 2011, 67–69).

These settings offer an alternative to the typical public hearings, which are formal, sometimes adversarial, and often held when the decision-making body has already decided what to do. In a participatory process, community leaders and public professionals engage with citizens, each listening to the ideas of others and learning about alternative ways to deal with current issues. Though there is the potential for imbalance and abuse when people with a particular agenda try to dominate the discussion, well-designed and -conducted citizen involvement systems can improve the quality of public decision making (Thomas 2012).

Not every government function lends itself to citizen participation in decision making, nor is a participatory process the best approach in all places and times. It can be effective when communities are dealing with issues that interest the public, there are multiple perspectives that are difficult to fully anticipate, and public buy-in to solutions is important to community success. In these situations, democracy becomes a key public service value, not just in the abstract as a concept taught in political science courses, but as a real and immediate part of daily community life.

For the public professional, this is not a matter of "pleasing the customer," in the language of the market paradigm of public administration. Instead, it is about serving as a facilitator for community dialogue, so that citizens are not only passive consumers of public service but also people who actively help decide what services will be offered and in what ways. This concept may not affect the legal structures of government under state constitutions and local laws, but it can change how elected leaders gather information about citizen preferences and formulate ideas for policies and projects.

Three useful concepts describing ways practitioners can facilitate community dialogue are the "listening bureaucrat," the "helper," and the "citizen in lieu of the rest of us." All three of these views of the role of the public professional support the value of democracy with values such as participation and openness.

Camilla Stivers (1994) describes listening to citizens as a practice that moves the public professional beyond the basic task of implementing policy. It "helps administrators glean important information, define situations more carefully, hear neglected aspects and interests, and facilitate just and prudent action in often turbulent environments" (368). According to Stivers, this "supports both democratic accountability and administrative effectiveness" by promoting "openness, respect for difference, and reciprocity" (367).

In the helper role described by Richard Box (1998), public professionals "take an active part in policy creation and implementation by serving to interpret public wishes for representatives, presenting professional knowledge of organizational and technical practices to citizens and representatives, and monitoring decision making and implementation to ensure that citizens have opportunities to participate" (139). Though helpers do not neglect professional tasks related to carrying out existing laws, policies, and programs, when they work with the public their "focus is on the process of dialogue and deliberation that leads to policy decisions and program implementation" (140).

Terry Cooper does not accept the idea that public administrators are by the nature of their work separated from the public at large. Instead, drawing on the writing of political philosopher Michael Walzer, Cooper (1991, 139) suggests that public professionals can serve as "citizens in lieu of the rest of us." Because they have available knowledge and access to governmental systems not readily available to the public, the "ethical identity of the public administrator then should be that of the citizen who is employed *as* one of us to work *for* us; a kind of professional citizen ordained to do that work which we in a complex large-scale political community are unable to undertake ourselves" (139). This concept recognizes the public professional's responsibility to elected leaders, but regards this as one source of responsibility, not the only source. Elected leaders, citizens, and public administrators are all involved in creating and implementing public policy. Cooper describes these relationships as a "dynamic iterative process" in which administrators

> should receive legislative direction from elected officials who are responsible for aggregating the wishes of their fellow citizens in the form of broad policies; bureaucrats then return to the citizenry for guidance in implementation; and, on other occasions, return to the politicians with recommendations from the citizenry for revisions and for new policies. Information, judgment, and advice flow back and forth around the circle of political authority. (140)

These are interesting role possibilities that use and enhance public service values, but there are many situations in which direct citizen involvement is not an option. Also, not everyone working in the public sector has opportunities to connect with citizens and take part in the policy-making process. Many public employees serve in positions in which values and the views of citizens are important, but working with the public would be unusual. In circumstances such as these, an alternative that incorporates the values of democracy, responsiveness, representativeness, and openness is the idea of "imagining private lives."

Richard Box (2011, 70) notes that "This is not a new idea and many people already do it." Imagining private lives involves using what public professionals know about conditions in society to shape policy recommendations and delivery of public services. It "is not an act of vague emotionalism, it is a matter of assembling knowledge gained through working with projects, problems, and conditions in the everyday work setting" (71). Using this technique, practitioners might ask questions such as "Could we make residents feel safer from street violence by changing our patrol strategy?" or "Can we increase successful outcomes with social services clients by focusing on individual circumstances rather than rules and processes?" (71).

CODES OF ETHICS AS A SOURCE OF VALUES

There are a number of codes of ethics in the public sector that include public service values (see Meine and Dunn [2013] for a survey of codes of ethics). There is only one—for ASPA—that applies across the entire sector, while the others come from professional associations based on specific occupations. The ASPA code is discussed below, but first we will examine the *Code of Ethics and Professional Conduct* of the American Institute of Certified Planners (AICP), which is part of the American Planning Association, using it as an example of an occupationally specific code.

Codes of ethics often contain aspirational statements and prescriptive rules of conduct. Aspirational statements express the association's ideals. They may not be entirely achievable, but they show the direction in which members want to take the profession; their purpose is to inspire. Prescriptive rules of conduct specify appropriate and inappropriate behaviors specific to the occupation. These are "do" and "don't" statements that define the role of members of the profession; if there is an enforcement mechanism for the code, they serve as the grounds for action.

The AICP code begins with an aspirational subsection, within a larger section labeled "Principles to Which We Aspire," that describes overall responsibility to the public. This subsection consists of an opening paragraph and eight statements:

AICP Code of Ethics and Professional Conduct

A. Principles to Which We Aspire
    1. Our Overall Responsibility to the Public
        Our primary obligation is to serve the public interest and we, therefore, owe our allegiance to a conscientiously attained concept of the public interest that is formulated through continuous and open debate. We shall achieve high standards of professional integrity, proficiency, and knowledge. To comply with our obligation to the public, we aspire to the following principles:
        a. We shall always be conscious of the rights of others.
        b. We shall have special concern for the long-range consequences of present actions.

c. We shall pay special attention to the interrelatedness of decisions.
d. We shall provide timely, adequate, clear, and accurate information on planning issues to all affected persons and to governmental decision makers.
e. We shall give people the opportunity to have a meaningful impact on the development of plans and programs that may affect them. Participation should be broad enough to include those who lack formal organization or influence.
f. We shall seek social justice by working to expand choice and opportunity for all persons, recognizing a special responsibility to plan for the needs of the disadvantaged and to promote racial and economic integration. We shall urge the alteration of policies, institutions, and decisions that oppose such needs.
g. We shall promote excellence of design and endeavor to conserve and preserve the integrity and heritage of the natural and built environment.
h. We shall deal fairly with all participants in the planning process. Those of us who are public officials or employees shall also deal evenhandedly with all planning process participants. (American Planning Association 2009)

This aspirational subsection is followed by two more, on "Our Responsibility to Our Clients and Employers" and "Our Responsibility to Our Profession and Colleagues." Then the code offers twenty-six rules of conduct, followed by a section on enforcement procedures. Here are two examples of the rules of conduct. Item 13 states, "We shall not sell, or offer to sell, services by stating or implying an ability to influence decisions by improper means." Item 18 reads, "We shall not direct or coerce other professionals to make analyses or reach findings not supported by available evidence" (American Planning Association 2009). These two statements express values of honesty and integrity in relationships with clients and in the use of knowledge gained in professional practice. We can see that these issues would be of particular interest to planning professionals, whose work involves interaction with decision-making bodies— thus the prohibition on claiming an ability to influence decisions by improper means—and interaction with other planners, involving the accurate and factual use of data.

It is in the aspirational subsection that we find concentrated attention to public service values. The opening paragraph mentions the public interest, integrity, proficiency, and knowledge. This is followed by a listing of the following principles describing members' "overall responsibility to the public":

- Consciousness of the rights of others;
- Concern for long-range consequences;
- Attention to the interrelatedness of decisions;
- Timely, adequate, clear, and accurate information;
- Broadly based citizen participation;
- Social justice, including the needs of the disadvantaged and racial and economic integration;
- Excellence of design;
- Preserving the integrity and heritage of the natural and built environment; and
- Fairness in dealing with participants in the planning process. (American Planning Association 2009)

Some of these values, such as social justice and the rights of others, could be applicable to many professional specializations. Several others, such as concern for long-range consequences and excellence of design, are tailored to planning. Overall, the reader comes away with a relatively clear idea of who these people want to be and how they think about their professional practice.

The ASPA *Code of Ethics* has been updated several times, most recently in 2013 (ASPA 2013). In the most recent revision, the ASPA code was shortened and supplemented with a separate set of "practices" in support (Appendix B). It is worth reproducing the code here to highlight the public service values it contains:

ASPA Code of Ethics

The American Society for Public Administration (ASPA) advances the science, art, and practice of public administration. The Society affirms its responsibility to develop the spirit of responsible professionalism within its membership and to increase awareness and commitment to ethical principles and standards among all those who work in public service in all sectors. To this end, we, the members of the Society, commit ourselves to uphold the following principles:

1. Advance the Public Interest. Promote the interests of the public and put service to the public above service to oneself.
2. Uphold the Constitution and the Law. Respect and support government constitutions and laws, while seeking to improve laws and policies to promote the public good.
3. Promote Democratic Participation. Inform the public and encourage active engagement in governance. Be open, transparent and responsive, and respect and assist all persons in their dealings with public organizations.
4. Strengthen Social Equity. Treat all persons with fairness, justice, and equality and respect individual differences, rights, and freedoms. Promote affirmative action and other initiatives to reduce unfairness, injustice, and inequality in society.
5. Fully Inform and Advise. Provide accurate, honest, comprehensive, and timely information and advice to elected and appointed officials and governing board members, and to staff members in your organization.
6. Demonstrate Personal Integrity. Adhere to the highest standards of conduct to inspire public confidence and trust in public service.
7. Promote Ethical Organizations. Strive to attain the highest standards of ethics, stewardship, and public service in organizations that serve the public.
8. Advance Professional Excellence. Strengthen personal capabilities to act competently and ethically and encourage the professional development of others. (ASPA 2013)

Taking the ASPA *Code of Ethics* and its practices together, we can create the following list of values that ASPA thinks are important for public service (in the order they appear in the practices):

Public interest	Due process
Respect constitutions and laws	Democratic participation
	Openness
Equality	Transparency
Fairness	Respect all persons
Representativeness	Social equity
Responsiveness	Equal treatment

Provide full information	Honesty
Integrity	Effectiveness
Courage	Efficiency
Compassion	Excellence
Benevolence	Competence
Optimism	Professionalism

At this point in our exploration of sources of public service values, none of the ASPA values are a surprise. We might think of something to add or different ways to word a particular value, but this list reflects many of the concepts we have encountered from other sources. ASPA's eight principles are indeed aspirational, and they are worded to apply across the many occupational specializations in the public sector.

PUBLIC SERVICE VALUES IN ACCREDITATION STANDARDS

It may seem strange in a chapter on the sources of public service values to focus on standards adopted by an organization that accredits a portion of the graduate programs in public affairs. However, accreditation standards are an expression of what faculties in these programs think students should know. The ideas discussed in graduate public affairs programs are likely to have some impact on actions taken by public sector professionals, so they can be important for our discussion of values.

Network of Schools of Public Policy, Affairs, and Administration (NASPAA) is the accrediting body for master's-level public affairs degree programs. Not all public affairs programs are, or choose to be, accredited by NASPAA, though many are. In 2009, NASPAA adopted a new set of standards that emphasizes public service values. There may have been implied values in NASPAA's earlier standards. However, making public service values a central feature of the accreditation system suggests that normative values are going to become even more important than they already have been in the creation of public policy and the everyday delivery of governmental services.

Here is the NASPAA statement of important public service values from the 2009 accreditation standards:

> Public service values are important and enduring beliefs, ideals and principles shared by members of a community about what is good and desirable and what is not. They include pursuing the public interest with accountability and transparency; serving professionally with competence, efficiency, and objectivity; acting ethically so as to uphold the public trust; and demonstrating respect, equity, and fairness in dealings with citizens and fellow public servants.

To accompany Bozeman's definition of values given in the section "A Specific Sort of Values" in Chapter 1, we have NASPAA's definition that is specifically tailored to public service values. These public service values are "enduring beliefs, ideas, and principles," they are "shared by members of a community," and they express what community members think is "good and desirable" and "what is not." The values are shown in four groups:

1. Pursuing the public interest with accountability and transparency.
2. Serving professionally with competence, efficiency, and objectivity.
3. Acting ethically so as to uphold the public trust.
4. Demonstrating respect, equity, and fairness in dealings with citizens and fellow public servants.

The first group is organized around the familiar *public interest*, connecting it with accountability and transparency. The second group includes values related to professional action and the third is about ethically correct behavior. In the fourth group, NASPAA combines three quite different concepts in describing the public professional's relationships with citizens and peers. The second concept, equity, is part of social justice, and fairness can be thought of as connected with values such as objectivity and neutrality.

To give each group a name that makes it easy to identify, we might use the following labels, in order: *accountability, professionalism, administrative ethics,* and *fairness.* Though this four-way categorization of values is not the same as Kernaghan's (discussed above in the section on value typologies), there are definite similarities. NASPAA's accountability group can be compared to Kernaghan's democratic category, both sets include professional and ethical values, and Kernaghan's people category can be paired with NASPAA's fairness group.

USING VALUES IN THE FIVE THEMATIC CHAPTERS

This chapter's overview of public service values shows that they are used by public service practitioners, academicians, and the faculty and administrators who accredit MPA programs. The values most in use in practice and research change over time, as some move in and out of favor and new ones are introduced during periods of reform or changes in schools of thought. Dialogue between students and faculty may also influence public service values, as students express views on values important to them, teachers offer related history and concepts, and the perceptions and daily work of each are changed by the interaction.

In this chapter, we have found remarkable agreement and consistency in public service values across quite different source materials. In the following five chapters, many of the values discussed in this chapter become part of the narrative associated with neutrality, efficiency, accountability, public service, and public interest.

APPENDIX A: VALUE DEFINITIONS FROM MOLINA AND MCKEOWN

The following list of public service values is quoted from Molina and McKeown (2012, 380):

Accountability To act willingly in justifying and explaining one's actions to relevant stakeholders

Benevolence To act in a manner that promotes good and avoids harm for citizens

Collegiality	To act loyally and show solidarity toward one's colleagues
Courage	To confront fear and act rightly in the face of personal risk
Dedication	To act with diligence, enthusiasm, and perseverance
Effectiveness	To act in a manner that best achieves the desired results
Efficiency	To act in a manner that achieves the desired results using minimal resources
Expertise	To act with competence, skill, and knowledge
Honesty	To act in a truthful manner and to comply with promises
Humaneness	To act in a manner that exhibits respect, compassion, and dignity toward others
Impartiality	To act without prejudice or bias toward particular individuals or groups
Inclusiveness	To act in a manner that includes citizens, customers, and other relevant stakeholders in the decision-making process
Incorruptibility	To act without prejudice or bias in favor of one's own private interests
Innovativeness	To act with initiative and creativity in introducing new policies or products
Integrity	To act in accordance with relevant moral values and norms
Lawfulness	To act in accordance with existing laws and rules
Obedience	To act in compliance with the instructions of superiors

Organizational Interest	To act in a manner that promotes the organization's interest
Participativeness	To act in a manner that promotes active citizen participation in administrative decision making
Pluralism	To act in a manner that seeks to accommodate the interests of a diverse citizenry
Profitability	To act in a manner that achieves financial gains for the organization
Public Interest	To act in a manner that promotes the public interest
Reliability	To act in a manner that is consistent, predictable, and trustworthy
Representativeness	To act in a manner that is consistent with the values of citizens
Responsiveness	To act in a manner that is in accordance with the preferences of citizens, customers, and other relevant stakeholders
Self-Interest	To act in a manner that promotes the well-being and professional development of the individual
Serviceability	To act in a manner that is helpful and provides quality service to citizens, customers, and other relevant stakeholders
Social Justice	To act in a manner that promotes a fair and just society
Sustainability	To act in a manner that seeks to protect and sustain nature and the environment
Transparency	To act in an manner that is open and visible to citizens, customers, and other relevant stakeholders

APPENDIX B: PRACTICES TO PROMOTE THE ASPA CODE OF ETHICS

The following statement was approved by the ASPA National Council on March 16, 2013.

The ASPA Code of Ethics (ASPA 2013) is a statement of the aspirations and high expectations of public servants. These practices serve as a guide to behavior for members of ASPA in carrying out its principles. The Code and these practices are intended to be used as a whole and in conjunction with one another. An ethical public servant will consider the full range of standards and values that are relevant to handling a specific matter and be committed to upholding both the spirit and the letter of this Code.

ASPA members are committed to:

1. Advance the Public Interest. Promote the interests of the public and put service to the public above service to oneself.
   a. Seek to advance the good of the public as a whole, taking into account current and long-term interests of the society.
   b. Exercise discretionary authority to promote the public interest.
   c. Be prepared to make decisions that may not be popular but that are in the public's best interest.
   d. Subordinate personal interests and institutional loyalties to the public good.
   e. Serve all persons with courtesy, respect, and dedication to high standards.

2. Uphold the Constitution and the Law. Respect and support government constitutions and laws, while seeking to improve laws and policies to promote the public good.
   a. Recognize and understand the constitutional, legislative and regulatory framework in which you work and fully discharge your professional roles and responsibilities.

    b. Promote constitutional principles of equality, fairness, representativeness, responsiveness and due process in protecting citizens' rights and promoting the public good.

    c. Develop proposals for sound laws and policies and for improving or eliminating laws and policies that are unethical, counterproductive, or obsolete.

    d. Respect and safeguard protected and confidential information.

3. Promote Democratic Participation. Inform the public and encourage active engagement in governance. Be open, transparent and responsive, and respect and assist all persons in their dealings with public organizations.

    a. Be open and transparent while protecting privacy rights and security.

    b. Recognize and support the public's right to know the public's business.

    c. Involve the community in the development, implementation, and assessment of policies and public programs, and seek to empower citizens in the democratic process, including special assistance to those who lack resources or influence.

    d. Assist members of the public in their dealings with government and respond to the public in ways that are complete, clear, and easy to understand.

    e. Promote timely and continuing dissemination of information about government activities to the community, ensuring a fair and transparent process and educating citizens to make effective contributions.

4. Strengthen Social Equity. Treat all persons with fairness, justice, and equality and respect individual differences, rights, and freedoms. Promote affirmative action and other initiatives to reduce unfairness, injustice, and inequality in society.

    a. Provide services to the public with impartiality and consistency tempered by recognition of differences. Ensure that all persons have access to programs and services to which they are entitled under the law and maintain equitable standards of quality for all who receive the programs and services.

b. Provide equal treatment, protection, and due process to all persons.

c. Oppose all forms of discrimination and harassment and promote affirmative action, cultural competence, and other efforts to reduce disparities in outcomes and increase the inclusion of underrepresented groups.

5. Fully Inform and Advise. Provide accurate, honest, comprehensive, and timely information and advice to elected and appointed officials and governing board members, and to staff members in your organization.

a. Provide information and advice based on a complete and impartial review of circumstances and needs of the public and the goals and objectives of the organization.

b. Be prepared to provide information and recommendations that may not be popular or preferred by superiors or colleagues.

6. Demonstrate Personal Integrity. Adhere to the highest standards of conduct to inspire public confidence and trust in public service.

a. Exercise integrity, courage, compassion, benevolence, and optimism.

b. Maintain truthfulness and honesty and do not compromise them for advancement, honor, or personal gain.

c. Resist political, organizational, and personal pressures to compromise ethical integrity and principles and support others who are subject to these pressures.

d. Accept individual responsibility for your actions and the consequences of your actions.

e. Guard against using public position for personal gain or to advance personal or private interests.

f. Zealously guard against conflict of interest or its appearance. Disclose any interests that may affect objectivity in making decisions and recuse oneself from participation in those decisions.

g. Conduct official acts without partisanship or favoritism.

h. Ensure that others receive credit for their work and contributions.

7. Promote Ethical Organizations: Strive to attain the highest standards of ethics, stewardship, and public service in organizations that serve the public.

a. Work to establish procedures that hold individuals and the organization accountable for their conduct and support these procedures with clear reporting of activities and accomplishments.

b. Act as stewards of public funds by the strategic, effective, and efficient use of resources; by regularly reexamining the efficacy of policies, programs, and services; and by seeking to prevent all forms of mismanagement or waste.

c. Encourage open expression of views by staff members within the organization and provide administrative channels for dissent. Protect the whistleblowing rights of public employees, provide assurance of due process and safeguards against reprisal, and give support to colleagues who are victims of retribution.

d. Seek to correct instances of wrongdoing or report them to superiors. If remedies cannot be assured by reporting wrongdoing internally, seek external sources or agencies for review and action.

e. Support merit principles that promote excellence, competence, and professionalism in the selection and promotion of public officials and employees and protect against biased, arbitrary, and capricious actions.

f. Promote proactive efforts to increase the representativeness of the public workforce and the full inclusion of persons with diverse characteristics.

g. Encourage organizations to adopt, distribute, and periodically review a code of ethics as a living document that applies principles of this code and other relevant codes to the specific mission and conditions of the organization.

8. Advance Professional Excellence: Strengthen personal capabilities to act competently and ethically and encourage the professional development of others.

   a. Keep up-to-date on emerging issues, practices, and potential problems that could affect your performance and accomplishing the mission of your organization.

   b. Provide support and encouragement to others to upgrade competence and participate in professional activities and associations.

   c. Allocate time and resources to the professional development of students, interns, beginning professionals, and other colleagues.

3

Neutrality

The Public Professional in a Democratic Society

The Idea of Neutrality in Public Service

This concept sounds boring—neutrality, the absence of values, but it is the standard against which public service professionals are judged in American society. The expectation is that public employees, because they are nonelected, serve without interjecting their values or preferences into the daily work of carrying out the decisions of elected representatives of the people. However, reality is not entirely like this, so there is conflict between the expected and actual role of the public professional. This conflict makes the idea of neutrality much more interesting; if this is what we are supposed to be, but facts on the ground make achieving it unlikely, how can the concept and the reality be reconciled?

Political neutrality is an ideal, an important way of thinking about how public professionals serve the people in a democracy. In the eighteenth century, when the American government was a new creation, its leaders belonged to the nation's elite, people committed to its success and willing to serve despite considerable inconvenience. These elected leaders were assisted by a few clerks and other office employees, and they supervised what by today's standards were small numbers of employees such as postmasters and military personnel. Given the size of government at the time, monitoring the activities of unelected employees to

51

be sure they were doing what they were supposed to do was not the problem it is today.

As government grew in the nineteenth century, the appointment of people with political loyalty to those in power was a primary means of controlling the actions of public employees. It became apparent that complexity and specialization called for a change in emphasis from political loyalty to education and technical training, so political neutrality emerged as an issue in government operations. If public employees were to serve multiple administrations without regard to political loyalties, how would their actions be controlled? They would not necessarily share the policy preferences of elected leaders, and, as agencies grew in size, it was no longer feasible to monitor the daily actions and attitudes of public employees.

The nineteenth century was the period of the Industrial Revolution, a dynamic time of national expansion; people moved to the cities to work in factories and large companies, railroads spread across vast distances, the West was settled by homesteaders, and science and technology were transforming society. The practices of organization and management in government had not kept pace with these changes. At the national level, patronage appointments based on political loyalty hampered efforts to improve efficiency, and political "machines" and corruption at the local level made it difficult to provide services that matched the challenges of rapid growth. It is not easy today for us to imagine what life in the cities was like in the late nineteenth and early twentieth centuries. Poor sanitation, crowding, the hazards of illness and disease, terrible working conditions, and unsafe food, were the everyday lot of residents of urban areas. Government did little to improve these conditions, and some public officials profited from kickbacks and bribes (Judd and Swanstrom 2011).

The inefficiencies and corruption of government at all levels inspired people to look for solutions grounded in science and technique, setting the stage for a contradiction between the wishes of politicians and the work of career professionals hired to carry out the policies that the politicians adopted. As the nation moved into the Progressive Era and the twentieth century, civil service and personnel systems with standardized written job requirements and procedures for hiring, promotion, and discipline became common. These systems formalized the expectation that public employees would carry out their duties according to laws adopted by majority rule rather than the political preferences of individual elected officials. Thus, the work of public professionals was neutral in relation to partisan politics and less subject to the outcome of elections. It could be influenced over the long term by changes in funding levels or policy emphasis, but its daily content was to a large extent insulated from political debate and the wishes of elected leaders. In turn, public employees were not expected to participate in shaping public policies or to interact with the public to influence public opinion.

The idea of political neutrality—public employees stay out of the policy process and politicians do not try to control daily administrative work—fits common public perceptions of bureaucracy and the role of public employees in society. Most citizens think that people who work in the public sector are given general directives by legislative bodies that they carry out without question. This is in keeping with representative democracy, in which the people as a whole elect citizens to serve as leaders who make laws, levy taxes, and ensure that public agencies function as they should. James Svara (2015, 47) describes the idea of a clear split between elected leaders and public professionals this way (Svara does not advocate this view; he is describing its pure form):

> There are legitimate concerns about ensuring that administrators do not operate outside a set of controls. They do not own their organization nor should they unilaterally determine its policies. This concern leads some to the extreme conclusion that administrators cannot be moral agents because of the role they fill. In this view, the public administrator is a narrowly neutral agent whose only options are to obey orders or resign from the organization. Administrators are seen to be so completely neutral that they are not supposed to make any value judgments, because such judgments are to be made by political superiors alone.

As we discuss below, the realities of daily practice present challenges to this view of political neutrality. Even so, in a democratic society it continues to be a standard against which other public service values are measured. To the extent values in practice have normative content that is not neutral, but instead they suggest particular positions or outcomes, they may seem to threaten the concept of democratic control of government by the people.

The sections immediately below describe the concept of a dichotomy between politics and administration, the legal and institutional boundaries surrounding public practice, and challenges to the idea of neutrality. Next, the values *obedience, expertise,* and *impartiality* are examined in detail as elements of neutrality. The chapter concludes with a discussion of applying the concept of neutrality in daily work life.

DISTINGUISHING BETWEEN POLITICS AND ADMINISTRATION

Students of public administration are familiar with the story of the "politics-administration dichotomy." The narrative of the story is that in the early years of the field, in the late nineteenth century, people wanted to separate the daily work of administration from political influence, because they thought that administration should be businesslike and technical rather than about personal relationships and individual gain. However, by the middle of the twentieth century, it was recognized that a clean separation between the two spheres was impossible. Because public professionals experience every day the effects of on-the-ground implementation of adopted laws and policies, they are well positioned to know how policies should be implemented or changed to fit existing conditions.

By the 1960s and 1970s, it was commonly accepted that the idea of a dichotomy was naive and inaccurate. It was recognized that public professionals understood the political context in which they worked and responded accordingly, they often suggested revisions to existing policies, and they sometimes collaborated with citizens to shape new policies and programs. This more complicated situation presented a challenge to the standard model of representative democracy by acknowledging that administration was not entirely politics-free and that supposedly "neutral" career practitioners were sometimes involved in shaping public policies. In fact, at the local level, it was apparent that a significant portion of policy innovation came from public professionals, often working together with elected officials.

This situation resulted in questioning of the idea of a dichotomy between politics and administration or, more accurately, recognition of a distinction between the roles of elected leaders and public professionals rather than a clear split between them. This is indeed a distinction between roles. The expectations of people who are elected by the people for a specific term to make laws and oversee the operation of a unit of government are by their nature different from the expectations of people with technical training who are hired to deliver public services. The politics-administration relationship is not so important for the many practitioners who do not interact regularly with elected officials or citizens. But for those who do, and for those who have opportunities to influence policy formulation and change, understanding this relationship can be key to success.

As an example of role differences, let us examine a scenario in which the governing body of a city of 100,000 people, consisting of the elected mayor and six city council members, adopts an annual budget item to have streets repaired, improved, or resurfaced. They will evaluate performance later in the budget year to see how much of the work has been completed. In their review of the budget, the mayor and council members discuss priorities based on street conditions and how much money to spend given other service needs citywide. If the work is outsourced to private firms, they are involved in approving the contracts of companies that were the successful bidders to do the work. During public hearings on the budget, they may hear from citizens who have specific concerns about street conditions in the city, and this public input may influence priorities for spending the funds available for street improvements.

This is the decision-making process we expect in a representative democracy. The residents of the city elect leaders to make decisions about community services, and the leaders do just that. What is not so apparent is the administrative work behind the decision, as well as the daily work of implementation. The professional staff in the Public Works Department will maintain an ongoing computerized monitoring system that records street conditions based on several criteria (age and depth of pavement, traffic loads, base material, etc.) as well as field observations. The staff will prepare a budget proposal for the mayor and council that is shaped by data on past annual expenditures and current street conditions, prioritizing the coming year's work. When the proposal is discussed in a public meeting, staff will answer technical questions and analyze the impacts of prioritization options.

When the governing body has heard from citizens, discussed priorities, made amendments as appropriate, and adopted the budget item specifying priorities and spending levels, if projects are to be contracted out the staff will prepare technical materials to solicit bids from firms that do this sort of work. The staff members will evaluate the bids received, making recommendations to the governing body on which to accept. When contracts are approved, they will monitor performance of the work to see that technical standards are followed and that disruption to traffic flow and adjacent businesses and residences is kept to a minimum. If the work is done by city employees, all the tasks of field supervision are performed by city professionals.

In a future year, staff may suggest to the mayor and council that the amount of money budgeted for street work should be higher or lower than it has been in recent years. Based on criteria for street conditions and input from citizens, the staff may say that, as a matter of policy, it would be good to change the amount spent on this service. If the suggestion is to increase expenditures, the governing body will be in the position of balancing street work against other service needs, such as water treatment, park maintenance, libraries, strategic and land-use planning, and so on.

The elected city leaders probably have only a general idea of what is going on behind the scenes to prepare for their decision-making process and to carry out the priorities adopted in the budget. But notice the interactions between professional staff, elected leaders, citizens, and private firms, and how staff are involved at every stage of the process: monitoring on-the-ground conditions, preparing a budget proposal, assisting during decision making, working with private firms, supervising the work, and making recommendations as needed for changes in policy in future years.

In this setting, what is "politics" and what is "administration"? It would seem the process would be politicized if one or more members of the governing body sought to influence the content of the budget proposal before it was submitted to the full council. However, the mayor is the elected leader of city government; would it be inappropriately political for her or him to consult with staff as they work on the proposal? If a member of the city council is aware of citizen concerns about the condition of a particular street, would it be inappropriately political to share that information with a member of the Public Works Department?

Conversely, we could probably agree that it would exceed the boundaries of the professional role for staff to rally support among citizens for increased expenditure on road work, since this is a representational and political function normally reserved for elected officials. But would it be too political for a staff member to approach the mayor early in the process to ask for support for increased expenditures?

This all seems a bit muddy, so maybe interactions during the implementation phase would offer a clearer distinction between politics and administration. Ordinarily, we think of implementation as belonging to public professionals rather than elected leaders. Continuing with the street maintenance example, most of the everyday activities unfold as we would expect, with city staff and contract employees doing the work. Suppose, though, there are delays along a particular street due to coordination problems with utility companies, scheduling conflicts with other work, or similar issues that arise with projects like this. The street is a busy commercial arterial, with well-established businesses on both sides. The street frontage is torn up due to the improvement project, and the inconvenience is causing some customers to choose other parts of town for their shopping. As the delay drags on for several weeks, business owners approach elected officials to complain and push for speedy resolution, so the mayor tells the department head that this issue should be given priority over other current and pending projects.

Though staff members may dislike what they perceive as interference, they realize that if this problem is not resolved quickly it will become a topic at public meetings and appear in the local media, making them appear inefficient and obstructionist. They may find some reserve funds, shift personnel, or negotiate changes in process with contractors or utility companies. As a result, the project is finished quickly and everyone is happy. Is this inappropriate political influence over administrative affairs, or is it an example of representative democracy working as it should?

The reader will notice that I have chosen a rather mundane, routine example—street maintenance—to make the point that elected officials and professional staff are involved in a cooperative effort, each with their unique roles but not clearly separated into two different spheres of activity. We could sharpen the question of political influence by choosing an issue over which the governing body is deeply divided, such as a major commercial and residential development that would strain city services and change the character of the community. In this situation, professional staff is obligated to offer full information on costs, impacts, and alternatives, though either or both of the council factions might not want to hear it. Pressure could be brought to silence or terminate staff people, and certain staff members might have to make difficult ethical decisions about their role in the decision-making process.

Or we could shift to other levels of government, examining issues such as affirmative action policies in state universities or national-level policy issues such as timber cutting in publicly owned forests or acquisition of expensive new military hardware systems. In these and similar situations, professional staff and elected leaders may be involved at any or all stages of information gathering, discussion of alternatives, public consideration of options, and program implementation. Again, the roles that elected leaders and staff play will be different, with different expectations about how they act and how they relate to each other. Even so, both need to be involved to move public action forward, because success depends on a blending of democratic responsiveness and technical expertise.

An interesting thing about the story of the politics-administration dichotomy is that to some extent it is an abstraction disconnected from the realities of practice. Yes, there was a time when corruption and patronage appointments were especially damaging to efficient and effective government administration, and these problems have decreased thanks in part to clearer definition in the roles of politicians and public professionals. However, there never has been a crisp, clearly defined "dichotomy"; professional staff has always been involved in aspects of policy making, and elected leaders have always taken an interest in performance and implementation.

Scholarly debates about politics and administration are somewhat beside the point, since there are, obviously, differences in the roles people play in policy making and implementation, and it is equally clear that an interdependent relationship is needed to make the process work. Who should be involved in which aspects in a given place and time will continue to be a question the people involved must sort out for themselves. Though there are role boundaries and expectations that most would agree should not be violated, they leave considerable room for variation and choice in public service.

BOUNDARIES AROUND DAILY PRACTICE

This discussion of politics and administration could leave us thinking there are few clearly defined borders around the professional role, little to serve as guide or restriction upon action except what seems to be acceptable to the people involved in a particular issue or project. Though there is some room for public professionals to choose their roles in particular situations, there are very real boundaries around those roles, boundaries that reinforce the concept of neutrality.

A term often used to describe a public professional's action options is "administrative discretion." To exercise administrative discretion is to choose a course of action by taking into account what is expected of a professional in a specific occupational role (such as a manager in a federal agency, a city police captain, or a state highway engineer) and in the particular circumstances at hand. These circumstances include the unit of government (national, state, or local; geographic area; types of services offered), the clientele and people who would be affected by the practitioner's action, and what organizational peers and superiors, elected officials, and citizens think it is appropriate for a person in this role to do. Exercising administrative discretion means to go outside defined or mandated actions required of a particular position, taking responsibility for choosing among alternatives.

When a public professional acts in ways that seem to fit her or his role, people may agree or disagree with what is done, but they will not worry that the actions are inappropriate. If, instead, people think some actions are not appropriate for professionals in that role, they may object or resist on those grounds alone. Over time, changes in the demands of the job and the expectations of those affected by a professional's actions may mean that the role itself expands, allowing additional possibilities for exercising administrative discretion.

We need to examine what it is that sets the boundaries around appropriate administrative discretion. How do we know what is appropriate, so that acting on one's values produces results that are appropriate for one's role? Four types of boundaries that are especially important in public service are discussed below, beginning at the general, macro level and moving toward the specific, micro level. The four types of boundaries are the Constitution, legislation, professional norms, and organizational expectations.

The Constitution

A constitution is the most general category of boundaries to administrative discretion, broadly applicable across all public organizations. Unlike boundaries composed of particular pieces of legislation that apply only in certain cases, or expectations for the behavior of public professionals that apply to specific occupations or individual units of government, a constitution determines the structure and functions of government, expressing a sense of purpose and cultural values.

Because it is somewhat distant from the daily workplace and seems abstract, it is easy to lose sight of the importance of the U.S. Constitution to the structure and function of government at all levels as well as the relationship between citizens and government. Sheila Kennedy and David Schultz (2011) write about a "constitutional ethic" that includes, among other things, a limited and divided representative government, protection of individual liberties, political equality and equality of opportunity, federalism (recognition of the role of state governments), rule of law rather than rule by individual preference, protection of the minority, pluralism (recognition of a multiplicity of views), and a secular government separated from any particular religious view. This constitutional ethic was created during the Age of Enlightenment, a time when some people were thinking for themselves using reason and science, instead of accepting what they were told to believe by governmental and religious authorities.

When the government of the United States was being shaped, *classical liberalism* was a major theme in political thought. Related to Enlightenment thought, classical liberalism is about individual freedom, not the sort of big-government liberalism that is debated today. It can be found, for example, in the vision of democracy that Thomas Jefferson expressed in the Declaration of Independence. Another political perspective important at that time was *classical republicanism*, which "favors society over the individual" (Box 2014, 24). Classical republicanism is not about a political party, but expresses the view that virtuous citizens place the good of the collective community over individual good. The U.S. Constitution reflects both these perspectives, protecting individual liberties while creating a national system of government that is much stronger than the one it replaced (the Articles of Confederation). These themes in American political culture remain current today; though the specific public issues are different from those of the early years of the nation, the tension between individual liberty and the good of the whole is as vibrant and dynamic now as it was then.

However remote the Constitution may seem from the everyday practice of public administration, its values express the core cultural beliefs of the people who created the nation and continue to both reflect and shape values in today's American society. This means that public professionals can find guidance in the constitutional ethic by examining its meaning as expressed, for example, through legislation, public dialogue over issues of public policy, and decisions of the U.S. Supreme Court (Rohr 1989). They can also use their knowledge of constitutional values to better understand the politics and debates over public policy that shape the organizational landscape of the contemporary public sector.

Legislation

In a governmental system based on law, legislation passed at the national, state, and local level is one of the most important boundaries to administrative action. When legislative bills become public laws, they create programs, establish budgets, and determine the legality of certain behaviors. These are powerful and important tools of government action in society. They reflect the values of the citizenry and their representatives, and they often have significant effects on the daily work life of public professionals.

A common concern in political science and public administration is that administrative agencies have too much discretion to choose a course of action because legislation is intentionally vague rather than specifically stating what is to be done. In the 1940s, Herman Finer argued that the actions of public administrators should be controlled by external means, since their internal, professional sense of what is right is insufficient to ensure compliance with the democratic will of the people (Denhardt and Denhardt 2011, 121–125). Theodore Lowi (1969) argues that Congress does not do enough to specify what it wants in legislation, instead granting too much authority to administrative agencies to decide how to implement the laws. Terry Cooper (2012, 53) puts it this way:

> The growing complexity and technical nature of problems addressed by government have created a tendency in legislators to delegate enormous powers to administrators, who are presumed to have specialized knowledge of particular policy areas. Thus the implementation of legislation becomes, in fact, an exercise in substantive policy making. Broad legislative "shells," debated publicly and approved by elected officials, are then filled with a multitude of administrative decisions that are far less visible and far more difficult to monitor. These bureaucratic rules and regulations become the real substance of public policies.

At the national and state levels of government, there are laws that prescribe how administrative agencies will create regulations that implement legislation (at the federal level, this is the Administrative Procedure Act of 1946). In local government, legislation (called "ordinances") can be quite specific, but here, too, there is often considerable room for interpretation and elaboration. If we add together all the laws that have been passed at all levels of government, it would be an impressively large collection. These laws convey the intent of the people's representatives and at least to some extent the will of a large percentage of the population of each governmental jurisdiction (city, county, state, and nation). They tell public professionals what they are expected to do and for what reasons, making them a primary source of boundaries for the administrative role.

Professional Values

We have seen in Chapter 2 that professional values are often expressed in codes of ethics. They can also be found in generally accepted practices, in articles on professional practice, and in related books. Herman Finer's argument for greater control of administrators through legislation is mentioned in the section above. Finer was engaged in a debate with Carl Friedrich, who thought "that the key to bureaucratic responsibility was professionalism" (Denhardt and Denhardt 2011, 122). According to Denhardt and Denhardt, from Friedrich's perspective, "administrators have to use their technical and professional knowledge in order to be responsible. Therefore, for a public administrator, being accountable means not only following the law and doing what you are told to do by elected officials, but also using the expertise of your profession" (124).

Friedrich was arguing for the importance of an individual's internal, personal boundaries on administrative discretion—professional values—in contrast with Finer's emphasis on externally imposed boundaries such as legislation. As we might expect, both professional values and external controls are important for work in the public sector. We need not worry too much here about which is more significant, since that balance will vary depending on the person and the situation. It will also vary depending on the particular occupation, as discussed earlier. The public sector includes many occupational specializations, each with its own set of professional values. Though we have identified public service values that apply across all public sector occupations, many others are occupation-specific.

To illustrate the significance of occupation-specific values to people who work in a particular field, we can use the *Code of Ethics* of the International City/County Management Association (ICMA). ICMA's code is decades old, it is well-known and respected in the city management profession, and it is enforceable; members who are found to have violated it can be disciplined or expelled from the association. The ICMA code consists of twelve "tenets," with guidelines (ICMA 2013). Tenet 3 reads: "Be dedicated to the highest ideals of honor and integrity in all public and personal relationships in order that the member may merit the respect and confidence of the elected officials, of other officials and employees, and of the public." Among the several guidelines to Tenet 3 is one that reads, "Members should not seek employment for a position having an incumbent administrator who has not resigned or been officially informed that his or her services are to be terminated."

City management is a little unusual, because there is only one manager in each city that has a city manager, they change jobs relatively frequently, and they are at-will employees, appointed by the governing body and dismissible at any time. Given these characteristics, we can understand why the managers' professional association prefers that members avoid asking about employment when another member is already in the position. The point for our discussion is that there are values associated with the city management profession, and one of them is this prohibition against a specific form of competition with other members.

Organizational Expectations

The expectations of people in one's own organization are an especially powerful form of boundaries around the professional role. They are immediately present every day, people use them to form impressions of public professionals and to evaluate their work, and they are enforced with rewards and punishments. They make it easier for a practitioner to work within the boundaries of a role, carrying out daily tasks in a way that appears neutral to other people in, or who interact with, the organization.

Organizational expectations are both written and unwritten. In written form, they include personnel rules and collective bargaining agreements, job descriptions, mission statements, administrative regulations, departmental policies, descriptions of work tasks and processes, and the content of websites. Unwritten expectations include the perceived preferences of organizational superiors; the stories coworkers tell about organizational events, personalities, and policies; and knowledge of the actions and policy preferences of elected governing bodies and political leaders.

Organizational expectations can be very effective as a means of supporting the value of neutrality. Look again at the list above of written expectations. Each item has an associated body of knowledge and practice, whether in the public sector as a whole (e.g., ways of constructing personnel rules or job descriptions) or in a given professional area of practice (such as mission statements and work tasks and processes in law enforcement, housing management, or wildlife management). These bodies of knowledge and practice are used to craft expectations specific to each organization, with their own unique histories, characteristics, and effects on the working environment of the organization's employees.

Each of the items in the list of unwritten expectations suggests a rich body of knowledge within individual organizations. People who join an organization will learn these things over time, which enables them to be more effective and reinforces conformity with the values and behavioral norms that other members of the organization believe to be appropriate.

CHALLENGES TO NEUTRALITY

Several aspects of professional work in the public sector make it difficult to remain neutral, to avoid showing preferences for the policy choices of particular groups or elected leaders. One of these is discussed above—the issue of vague legislation requiring administrative interpretation to be implemented. Here are some additional ways that the characteristics of the role of the public professional, and the professional commitments and values of practitioners, make it challenging to maintain a sense of policy neutrality.

The first way may be the most obvious: the on-the-ground conditions of the daily working environment give career professionals detailed knowledge of citizen needs, physical conditions, and financial circumstances of program implementation that few citizens or elected leaders will have. Sometimes, an elected leader or political appointee will have specialized knowledge in a particular area, but in many cases, it is career professionals who are best informed about existing conditions. When the time comes for operations to be reviewed or policies to be revised, it makes sense for political leaders to consult career practitioners. As a result, some public professionals will be involved in assisting with policy formulation and evaluation of existing policy to determine whether it should be revised.

Second, professional knowledge is not only based on observation and experience, but often grounded in education specific to the occupational role. Many public professionals have educational credentials that give them specific technical skills others do not have, and sometimes education provides a broad and informed view of the area of practice that is useful in a leadership role.

Third, at times it seems that elected leaders, whether a legislative body or a single elected head of government, are not representing the wishes of the people. They may take policy positions that seem destructive to the long-term public interest, or they may hold political views that are out of the mainstream to the point that it appears damage is being done. This *failure of representation* may prompt public professionals to soften, delay, or redirect the effects of the politicians' seemingly misguided action. For example, suppose the members of the city council of a large coastal city will not recognize the coming impacts of climate change and plan for it. City staff with technical backgrounds in engineering, land-use planning, and public safety may think this neglect is grossly irresponsible, putting lives and properties at unnecessary risk. There are action alternatives available to address this problem, and the sooner they are implemented, the less severe the damage would be from storms and a rise in sea level.

The question is what the concerned staff people might do, since the governing body will not act. The value of neutrality suggests that public professionals should give the governing body the available information on estimates of sea level rise, storm damage, financial consequences, and potential solutions, and then stand by as the elected leaders decide what actions the city will take, if any. In this case, however, the staff has already done that and the city council has rejected its advice. Members of the governing body are the representatives of the people and the employers of city staff; in a democratic system, if the people are not pleased with the decisions of elected officials, they can replace them at an election. However, in our hypothetical city, which is not unlike many cities, election turnover in council seats is low, so that council members may serve for many years, and the people of the city are mostly ill-informed and apathetic about local public issues.

There are a number of things staff might do in this situation, if they choose not to remain neutral. Here are three options; the first does not move very far away from the neutral ideal, while the third could be perceived as quite political. The first option is to work on staff-level planning for future challenges due to water incursion. This activity could be portrayed as just another part of the city's planning for infrastructure improvements and emergency preparedness. Whether council members would accept this view of the activity remains to be seen. However, if the time comes when the reality of sea level rise is difficult for the politicians to deny, staff would have a body of work ready to support policy implementation.

Another option, in addition to planning, would be to coordinate with other agencies at the county, state, and local levels, along with nonprofit organizations, on long-range land-use and emergency management planning. It would be difficult to hide this involvement from council members, but interagency coordination is a normal part of the roles of public professionals, so perhaps it would be accepted. The third option is more aggressive. In addition to the first two options, staff could actively share their planning work with local organizations (Chamber of Commerce, businesses with large facilities in possible flood zones, universities, neighborhood associations, the local media, and so on). This might generate political pressure on the council to reverse its position and actively pursue protecting the city. It might also be perceived as anti-democratic, insubordinate, and a direct challenge to the governing body—this could result in strained relations between staff and elected leaders and/or termination of key employees. Thus, we find that deviating from the neutrality ideal has the potential for significant public good, but also for generating conflict over the role of public professionals in a democratic society.

Finally, a fourth way the role of the public professional can make it challenging to maintain a sense of policy neutrality is professional value commitments. Depending on specific situations, holding a serious commitment to public service values such as transparency, the public interest, or citizen involvement in governance could make it difficult to stay out of discussions about the content of potential policies or changes to existing policies. This challenge to neutrality parallels the challenge due to failure of representation, but failure of representation need not be present; instead, the wish to participate in discussions due to value commitments can occur during typical policy design processes in which elected leaders engage with the public over the advantages and disadvantages of policy options. Again, though, this participation strains the meaning of neutrality, because nonelected professionals are acting on their values to influence policy outcomes.

VALUES ASSOCIATED WITH NEUTRALITY

At the end of Chapter 2, we noted that some of the values identified in the discussion of sources of public service values would be discussed further in later chapters. There are several public service values related to neutrality and three of them seem particularly important: *obedience, expertise,* and *impartiality.* The first, obedience, is about implementing adopted policies, laws, and instructions of elected officials and organizational superiors largely without question. The values *duty* and *loyalty* express related concepts of carrying out the lawful directives of elected representatives as they are given.

The word "obedience" has an odd sound to it; the reader may be forgiven for thinking of slavish adherence to the orders of a dictator or even obedience training for a pet dog. Nevertheless, it is a clear, unambiguous way of describing the extent to which public professionals comply with directives of political superiors. Use of obedience as a value in daily professional work must be accompanied by the reservation that policies or procedures contained in a directive must not be illegal or in some way grossly damaging to the public. Also, loyalty to one's organization is not the same thing as loyalty to a particular political party, ideology, or policy orientation that may characterize the current members of an elected governing body (Congress, state legislature, local council, or board) or executive leader (president, governor, mayor, or board chairperson). One may be loyal to the organization without violating the concept of neutrality by favoring a specific political orientation. Taking those factors into account, obedience expresses a rather pure form of neutrality, carrying out directives in a way that is as close to the intent of elected or appointed political leaders as it can be.

The public service value expertise is easy to identify with, since a key feature of contemporary professional bureaucracy is that its members have expert knowledge of specific public services. Moving from patronage appointments (people hired for government positions based on political loyalty rather than qualifications) to merit-based employment was a primary goal of those who worked to reform the public sector during the late nineteenth century and early twentieth century. For public sector jobs that require only a minimal background of education and experience, the absence of expertise may not be critical. However, public employees at all levels of government include a significant percentage of people with related education and specialized experience, so expertise is important.

Even a value this constructive and important can have disadvantages and potentially negative features. There can be tension between democracy and expertise if public professionals with expert knowledge exclude the public from accessing, understanding, and discussing information and ideas related to public issues and from meaningfully participating in the formulation or revision of public policies. Dwight Waldo (1980, 176–177) describes the democracy-expertise tension as a conflict between two types of authority, the authority of democratic representation and the authority of knowledge. Daniel Yankelovich (1991, 5) advocates "enhancing the quality of public judgment" as a way of countering the tendency of expertise to crowd out democracy, calling this tendency "creeping expertism." For Thomas McCollough (1991, 60–61), the key to resolving the democracy-expertise tension is to make value choices "open to critical debate by the political community." If they are not, "government becomes rule by experts" (61).

These concerns do not negate the importance of expertise in running the contemporary government, and there are good ways to make democratic self-governance and expertise compatible. As Yankelovich (1991, 242–243) notes, "In practice, however, it makes no sense to weaken the experts. A populist, antiexpert, anti-intellectual rampage might give some activists emotional satisfaction. But it would be short-lived. . . . Given the nature of modern industrial society, to discourage the experts from making their optimum contribution would be mindlessly self-destructive." When nonelected public professionals with expertise seem to dictate to the public or are out of touch with on-the-ground realities, the public may protest and ask for greater democratic, political control of administration. However, the public sector depends on expertise and in most situations the relationship of experts and citizens is positive.

Impartiality means acting with fairness and without prejudice or bias toward particular individuals or groups. It can be difficult to establish a public perception of impartiality when citizens have preconceptions about bias by government or when political leaders have particular preferences they want administrative agencies to promote. If certain people or populations have been excluded, ignored, or damaged by the way a particular public policy has been implemented, moving toward practices that are fairer and more impartial can benefit the value of social justice.

On the other hand, if public services or resources are already allocated on an equal and impartial basis, but the need is greater among some people than it is for others, impartiality may promote inequality and a perception of unfairness. As an example, school district staff may allocate the same annual budgetary amount per student in a wealthy area and in a poor area, thinking this is fair. However, parents in wealthy neighborhoods are able to contribute additional resources for classroom electronics, building improvements, and other extras that people in the poor area cannot afford. In addition, school facilities in poor neighborhoods may be old and in a deteriorated condition, and security there may not be adequate to keep children safe. In this situation, impartiality as a value is in conflict with social justice. It may be that administrators who think about this situation from the perspective of multiple values will decide to shift some resources to the poor area of the district.

Impartiality is an important way to think about avoiding bias generated by political power, mistreatment of people who have little political influence, improper financial conflict of interest, and other problems that can appear in the public sector. As with many values, it is most useful when we think about it in relation to other values, realizing there can be trade-offs between them that help in achieving a balanced approach.

APPLYING NEUTRALITY IN PROFESSIONAL LIFE

This chapter began with the observation that "political neutrality is an ideal" and that Americans judge public professionals against that ideal. We have examined role boundaries that reinforce neutrality, challenges to the ideal, and related values. The current environment of the public sector includes changes in the demographics of the population, rapid advances in technology, demands for citizen participation in creating and implementing policy, and working with outside groups such as contractors, nonprofit organizations, and other public agencies. These realities of contemporary practice make it more difficult than ever to remain value neutral, to carry out law and policy without appearing to favor particular views.

Reconciling the value of neutrality as an ideal with what public professionals know of practice means in part distinguishing between attaching themselves to specific political leaders or perspectives and expressing their best professional judgment. James Svara (2015, 48) puts it this way:

> Administrators should be neutral, but administrative neutrality means not taking sides and supporting some political superiors over others. Neutrality between parties, groups, or contenders for office does not preclude expressing value preferences, nor does it remove the obligation to display honesty and independence; "to speak truth to power."

It is not easy to sort out the difference between favoring particular perspectives and responsibly following one's professional judgment. This requires recognizing that pure neutrality is elusive in the real world, and that other values are important as well. Christoph Demmke and Timo Moilanen (2012, 8) capture the complexity of this situation well:

> Today, the role and limitation of the ethics of neutrality is largely recognized. It is accepted nowadays that individual behaviour is not only determined by rules and policies. Instead, it is also largely influenced by cultural aspects, leadership, fairness perceptions and feelings such as hope, fear, aspirations, etc. Therefore, ethical laws, principles, and standards do not cover all areas of human actions, nor do they always help in dealing with ethical dilemmas and personal conflicts. This also suggests that ethically good or acceptable behaviour can be defined not only by focusing on obedience to rules but encompasses also such issues like justice and fairness, leadership, ethical culture and the broader social context of behaviour.

Though it is reasonable to hope that elected leaders, political appointees, and public professionals will observe the expected boundaries of the roles they play in governing, we need to recognize that boundaries can become fuzzy. The challenge is not to deny or ignore this fact of organizational life, but to find ways to respond that are constructive for the public while remaining consistent with public service values. In the next chapter, we discuss a powerful and pervasive influence on public service values, the economic environment of the public sector.

4

Efficiency

The Economic Environment of Public Service

EFFICIENCY AS A PRIMARY VALUE

Borrowing from Molina and McKeown (2012), we can define efficiency as achieving desired results while using as few resources as possible. This value has always been central to government, even when it has been ignored or violated in practice. The wasteful and corrupt practices of the era of machine politics, spoils, and patronage hiring in the nineteenth and twentieth centuries did not meet our definition of efficiency. This is also true of some current practices in contracting services, acquisition of major weapons systems, abuses in social service programs, and so on. Nevertheless, people in government, whether elected leaders or staff, know that they *should* work with efficiency in mind, even when they are not doing so.

Public agencies do not operate in a vacuum, separated from the larger society, remaining "pure" and unaffected by what is happening outside. Instead, in a society characterized by a mixed economy in which government partially regulates the activities of a free market, we can expect market values to spill over to influence the public sector as well. This has always been true, but in the past three decades, the influence of market values on government has intensified, with phenomena such as reinventing, outsourcing, downsizing, rightsizing, quality circles, Total Quality Management, entrepreneurism, performance management, and New Public Management (NPM) (which includes elements of the others).

Economic efficiency is what the public wants from government, it is foundational to the private sector, and it is a dominant value in American society. As we found in Chapter 2, though public professionals are surrounded by societal expectations to make government "run like a business," their values continue to be those most directly connected to the traditional role of the public service practitioner in a democratic society, such as honesty, integrity, accountability, and dedication.

How can we bring together a personal commitment to values of public service and the reality of the dominance of economic thought and action in society? This chapter takes a realistic look at the efficiency-oriented society and the place of public administration in that society. The purpose is not to leave the reader feeling that it is pointless to care about public service values other than efficiency or that efficiency should be ignored, but instead to suggest ways that efficiency can be compatible with other values of public service. We are surrounded with the language and the values of economics and efficiency. Here, we explore a way to think of other public service values as important to "softening the sharp edges" of economic society, by injecting a sense of community and shared mission.

Our exploration of efficiency as a public service value begins with the opposition in American thought between *private interest* and *public purpose*, or individualism and community. It then turns to an examination of how efficiency became a dominant theme in the public sector several decades ago and a description of competing ideas that have become prominent in recent years. Following a case study assessing what is gained and what is lost by the focus on efficiency, we discuss associated values (*profitability, innovativeness, responsiveness,* and *serviceability*) and consider how efficiency as a value can be applied in professional work.

PRIVATE INTEREST AND PUBLIC PURPOSE

The American historical experience of breaking free from the dictates of church and monarchy was grounded in an ethic of individualism, a wish to protect each person from interference by institutions and other citizens. This historical experience resulted in a national government with divided, checked, and limited powers and state governments with considerable autonomy. The purpose was to limit the power exercised by any elected official, branch of government, or level of government and to prevent abuse of those who were in the political minority. Today, in a large urban, technological society, there are times when the complexity, competition between groups, and fragmentation in this structure seems to make decision making and action difficult.

This setting offers opportunities for people, groups, and organizations with resources to exercise considerable influence on the public sector, using it to benefit themselves at the expense of others. James Madison and his colleagues in the generation that wrote the Constitution hoped to avoid concentrations of power that would allow especially strong "factions" (what we would call parties or interest groups) to dominate others. This was a promising idea in the largely rural America of the late eighteenth century, but a technologically connected global economy has made it less feasible in the twenty-first century. The politics and policies of the contemporary public sector contribute to growing economic inequality and a sense that American democracy—at the national level, if not in many local communities—is suffering from citizen mistrust and dissatisfaction (King and Rank 2011; Krugman 2007).

Conflicts between private power and the interests of the public as a whole are not new. Though American culture is individualistic, Americans also express a wish for community, a sense of larger purpose, and a desire to take action that will benefit others and later generations.

Historian Arthur Schlesinger (1986) argues that the United States goes through cycles in which "private interest" dominates, followed by periods of "public purpose." According to Schlesinger, during periods of private interest people focus on their personal life circumstances; at the macro level, pursuit of profit and reduced public regulation of the private economy are emphasized. Over time, "materialism, hedonism, and the overriding quest for personal gratification" produce undercurrents of dissatisfaction, criticism, ferment, protest. Segments of the population fall behind in the acquisitive race. . . . Problems neglected become acute, threaten to become unmanageable and demand remedy. People grow bored with selfish motives and vistas, weary of materialism as the ultimate goal. The vacation from public responsibility replenishes the national energies and recharges the national batteries. People begin to seek meaning in life beyond themselves. (Schlesinger 1986, 28–29)

This description of periods of private interest fits the Gilded Age of the 1890s, with its rapid industrialization, formation of monopolies, and great inequality. It fits the Roaring Twenties, which were characterized by largely unchecked growth and speculation in the private sector, ending in economic collapse and the Great Depression. It fits the 1950s, during which the middle class expanded, many white people moved to the new suburbs, and for the first time it was expected that many people would work for large organizations instead of independently or in small companies. And it fits the 1980s, a time of anti-government sentiment, tax cuts for the wealthy, a shift in overall wealth to the top of the income distribution, and deregulation of business accompanied by a crisis in the savings and loan industry.

The first three of these periods of private interest were followed by periods of intense collective, public action: the Progressive Era, the New Deal, and the Great Society. The Gilded Age of the late nineteenth century was characterized by huge concentrations of wealth in the hands of a few. Some of the reforms of the Progressive Era were intended to reduce the effects of this level of inequality, by improving the living and working conditions of ordinary people and regulating large private firms. The social welfare measures introduced during the Great Depression of the 1930s and those of the Great Society years of the 1960s were also designed to counter widespread poverty, racism, and hardship amid concentrations of wealth and power. In addition to addressing social conditions and economic inequality, initiatives during these periods sought to protect the physical environment from damage created by the use of natural resources (such as forests, minerals, and wildlife) and from the effects of rapid industrial and urban development.

All of these transitions were accompanied by political and social turmoil, debate, and disagreement. In each case, the public at large was worried by the accumulation of wealth and power by a few people and private organizations. Measures to change the balance between the few and the many were met by accusations that the proponents were socialists, or communists, or un-American, determined to destroy the country. Today, we take for granted a workweek of reasonable length, prevention of child labor, safe food and drugs, the national park system, limits on corporate monopolies, the right of women to vote, income and medical support for older people, a "safety net" for those in need, civil rights protections, clean air and water, and so on. However, each of these collective actions and more were regarded by many as radical and unacceptable departures from conventional thought when they were proposed. A primary argument against many of them was economic—they would supposedly cost too much, damage the economy, cause inefficiency.

The balance between private interest and public purpose in the United States is different from that in many other developed countries. Few nations remain that have a dictatorial governance system where private ownership is limited and production is directed by governmental authorities. Many developed nations have a system commonly called "social democracy," in which a strong private sector is combined with a public sector reflecting citizen values that include protections and support for citizens, and often the physical environment, that are significantly greater than those in the United States.

Today, in the early part of the twenty-first century, the trend in the balance between private interest and public purpose is unclear. Beginning in the 1980s, private interest became more important in society and this trend was reflected in the public sector, with initiatives to downsize and limit the powers of government. Though there have been examples of public purpose in the following decades, as a generalization private interest has remained particularly important and efficiency has been emphasized in the public sector.

This has never been a matter of either private interest or public purpose, but instead a dynamic relationship in which both are present and the emphasis changes over time. In addition, it is not necessarily true that private interest and efficiency are compatible but public purpose and efficiency are not. Many public-sector programs and services are carried out efficiently and sometimes application of market techniques in the public sector produces inefficient results—a good example is contracting out, where in some cases cost overruns or inadequate performance are a problem.

Today, socioeconomic inequality has risen to a level unknown since the Gilded Age, national politics have become deeply polarized, and state and local governments are increasingly becoming sites of new initiatives in policy and governing. In the middle of this societal change and debate about the role of government in society, public professionals seem to remain focused on enduring values of public service, dealing with the shifting political and economic environment as best they can.

How Efficiency Became so Important

We know that economic efficiency has become especially important in the public sector since the 1980s, but why did this happen, and what has it meant for public service values? The development of economic theory in the U.S. public sector began in the 1950s— its rise to prominence is an interesting story of theory, politics, and practice coming together to produce significant change.

The public sector has experienced many "reforms" since public administration became an identifiable field of study in the late nineteenth century. Reforms are usually intended to increase efficiency, or effectiveness, or both. They are supposed to do this by improving the characteristics of leadership or management, or by improving the rigor and accuracy of planning, implementation, and outcomes measurement. Well-known examples include the council-manager format of local government organization beginning in the early twentieth century, POSDCORB (planning, organizing, staffing, directing, coordinating, reporting, budgeting) from the 1930s, PPBS (planning, programming, and budgeting system) beginning in the 1960s, and ZBB (zero-based budgeting) in the 1970s.

In addition to the United States, in the 1980s economic theory influenced public policy and management in nations such as Great Britain, New Zealand, Australia, and some European countries, spreading to many places globally by the 1990s. In some countries, such as New Zealand, this resulted in major restructuring and downsizing of the public sector. This reform impulse was unlike many earlier efforts, in two ways. First, it was oriented around the broad idea of using economics in the public sector, or "running government like a business." The assumption was that the public sector is inefficient and the private sector is efficient, so it should be good to bring market-like management techniques into the public sector. This idea—make government more like the private sector—allowed room to draw many different concepts into what was labeled *New Public Management* (NPM) in the 1990s. Some earlier reforms were also grounded in economic logic, but this one proposed reorienting the public sector as a whole.

Second, this wave of reform has lasted for decades. Many reforms become hot topics in professional associations, among politicians, and in academia, but then fade away in a few years, leaving behind some useful techniques and language that become a permanent part of management practice. The idea of using market logic in the public sector began in the 1950s, broke into public view in the United States during the Reagan years of the 1980s, and was put into daily practice during the Clinton years of the 1990s; only now, well into the twenty-first century, is the present time being characterized as "post-NPM." However, even in this supposedly post-NPM era, decades of applying economic concepts have significantly reshaped the public sector.

In the 1990s, the full extent of the global impact of economic theory on the public sector became apparent. During the Reagan administration in the 1980s, economic theory primarily supported macro-scale measures involving privatization, contracting out, cutting taxes, "devolving" central government services to lower levels, and so on. In the 1990s, scholars wrote about both this broad restructuring and "managerialist" techniques being used to move public organizations away from the standard characteristics of bureaucratic hierarchies. Janine O'Flynn (2007, 354) described the situation this way:

At the end of the 20th century, a postbureaucratic paradigm of public management was firmly embedded in many countries reflecting the outcome of the suite of reforms intended to enact a break from the traditional model of public administration underpinned by Weber's (1946) bureaucracy, Wilson's (1887) policy-administration divide, and Taylor's (1911) scientific management model of work organisation. In part at least, NPM was a reaction to perceived weaknesses of the traditional bureaucratic paradigm of public administration (O'Flynn 2005a; Stoker 2006), and it encompassed a "critique of monopolistic forms of service provision and an argument for a wider range of service providers and a more market-oriented approach to management" (Stoker 2006, 45). In articulating this NPM paradigm in the early 1990s, Hood set out its key doctrinal components (1991, 4–5): 1. Hands-on professional management; 2. Explicit standards and measures of performance; 3. Greater emphasis on output controls; 4. Disaggregation of units in the public sector; 5. Greater competition in the public sector; 6. Private sector styles of management practice; and 7. Greater discipline and parsimony in resource use.

In the United States, political leaders and public professionals became aware that something quite new was happening in government with the release of David Osborne and Ted Gaebler's book, *Reinventing Government: How the Entrepreneurial Spirit Is Transforming the Public Sector*, in 1993. Osborne and Gaebler described and promoted what they believed was a major transformation underway in American government. Among other themes, Osborne and Gaebler advocated using government to *steer* service delivery by others instead of *rowing* by doing it with government personnel, they wanted to inject *competition* into deciding who would deliver public services, they would measure *outcomes and impacts* instead of resource inputs, citizens would be viewed as *customers* to be given the public services they want, and government managers would be *entrepreneurial*, cutting costs and finding ways to make profits.

These concepts had been elements of NPM for some time, but the idea of reinventing government gave them popular appeal and NPM became a hot topic in government management, spreading into the Clinton administration's National Performance Review program and the "Congressionally driven" Government Performance and Results Act (Denhardt and Denhardt 2011, 16–20). In retrospect, we know that many reform concepts gathered easily under the umbrella of NPM, including both restructuring the role of government and shifting from classical bureaucratic management to an entrepreneurial style. Not all features of NPM were newly imported from the private sector; concepts such as budget cutting, accounting for performance, strategic planning, and rational instead of bureaucratic management were already found in the public sector prior to NPM (Gruening 2001).

The common feature of all these ideas is a calculative, efficiency-based logic drawn from the private market. Judy Whitcombe (2008, 8) offers a summary:

> NPM consists, essentially, of two sets of ideas: economics-based theories and managerialist systems. The theories which initially underpinned NPM, public choice theory and agency theory, and transaction-cost analysis had their origin in the discipline of economics and were referred to as the "new institutional economics" (Boston, 1996). Public choice theory had an influence on institutional design in a number of jurisdictions, and the application of one aspect resulted in the restructuring of government sector agencies to separate policy ministries from operational departments. Agency theory clarified the relationship between principals and agents and focused on accountability relationships. In New Zealand it was used to codify the relationship between chief executives and ministers under the State Sector Act 1988. The other component of NPM was the managerialism movement, which imported generic private sector management practices into the public sector in order to improve performance and increase efficiency and accountability.

It is not important to explore each relevant school of economic thought here, but we can contrast the market-based economic perspective with a "public interest" perspective. The economic way of thinking about the role of government in society is the opposite of that advocated by people who emphasize community, collective dialogue and decision making, and the public interest. The economic perspective focuses on the individual as a self-contained decision-making unit with a predetermined set of preferences, while the perspective involving the collective public interest envisions groups of people learning about alternatives and hearing the views of others, potentially finding solutions they had not considered in advance.

We have seen that NPM reforms address both government restructuring (taxes, privatization, etc.) and entrepreneurial management. Here is an example of the application of economic thought to the public sector that analyzes structures at the local, metropolitan level, with implications for ways that people approach issues of policy and management. In the Los Angeles metropolitan area, suburban cities surround the original central city. Only a fraction of the people in the Los Angeles area live in Los Angeles proper: the population in 2010 of the City of Los Angeles was approximately 4 million people, there were 13 million people in the Los Angeles metropolitan area, and there were 18 million people in the greater urban region. A map of the Los Angeles area shows that the central city is surrounded by dozens of other cities. What people often think of as one place is instead a complex metropolitan area composed of many urban places.

Each of these cities has a unique set of demographic, physical, political, and economic characteristics. Applying the economic perspective to this metropolitan setting, people decide where to live by choosing between "packages" of services offered by each city (schools, infrastructure, shopping areas, levels of taxation, etc.). In this way, the urban region functions like a market, with residents calculating the advantages and disadvantages of competing service packages offered by communities. When one place no longer serves a person's needs, she or he can move to another.

This image of the urban area as a marketplace of communities competing for residents does not adequately take into account the difficulties of moving from place to place. Not everyone finds it easy or desirable to leave one place for another; people have ties such as friends and children in school, and the range of choices available to low-income people is very limited. Nevertheless, this perspective calls our attention to how economic efficiency can influence development of urban areas. While the public interest perspective would focus on mutual issues and solutions to problems among the cities in the urban area, the economic perspective is particularly interested in competition, cost efficiency, and individual choice as forces shaping the metropolitan area. The motivations and policy preferences of public professionals might be different if they think of themselves as competing with other places than if they think of themselves as working collectively with citizens in their communities and with other cities to address joint problems.

Beyond NPM

It is no surprise that a reform agenda as broad and far-reaching as NPM has generated some concern and criticism. At the level of the relationship of the public sector to society, there is concern that treating citizens as customers diminishes democracy (Box et al. 2001). Also, moving from "rowing" to "steering" by contracting out public services, as advocated by Osborne and Gaebler (1993), may limit accountability and citizen influence in policy making (Denhardt and Denhardt 2011). At the level of organizational management, networked collaboration between public agencies and with the nonprofit and private sectors may be more effective than entrepreneurism and competition (Koliba, Meek, and Zia 2011; Terry 1998).

The overarching theme of these critiques is that values important to the public sector can be slighted or ignored by concentrating primarily on economic efficiency:

> For people who are concerned about the quality of public service and attention to issues of social injustice, fairness in governmental action, environmental protection, and so on, something about running government like a business does not feel right. It seems to degrade the commitment to public service, reducing it to technical-instrumental market functions not unlike the manufacture and marketing of a consumer product. Gone is the image of citizens determining public policy and its implementation to shape a better future, because customers do not actively participate in governance but wait passively to respond to an "agenda set by others" (Schachter 1997, 65). (Box 1999, 19–20)

In focusing on efficiency, "public entrepreneurs of the neo-managerialist persuasion are oblivious to other values highly prized in the U.S. constitutional democracy. Values such as fairness, justice, representation, or participation are not on the radar screen" (Terry 1998, 198). The idea of public interest does not fit well within the market model, because public interest is based on collective decision making and public purpose. In contrast, in the market model, decisions on policy and practice are made by aggregating individual preferences to please the "customers" of government.

NPM originated in response to "traditional" public admin-istration. In much the same way, the concepts of networks, governance, and citizen engagement being discussed today are responses to the market-based approach. The word "traditional" is in quotation marks because networks, governance, and citizen engagement were features of public administration before the arrival of NPM. They are not new, and public administration as study and practice has been comfortable with them for a long time. Nevertheless, because of changes in politics, economics, and demographics, the effects of NPM on the public sector in many nations, and the dynamics of technology and globalization, the trends emerging today take on an appearance of something new and uncharted.

In discussing most public service values, it is not necessary to emphasize balance and moderation or to remind the reader that other values are also important along with the one being discussed. Efficiency is different, though. Because the movement toward applying economics to the public sector made efficiency dominant among public service values, maintaining a sense of balance means that whenever we think about values we need to know that other values may be as important, or more important, in a particular situation. There is a difference between consider-ing efficiency in the design and implementation of services and making it the primary purpose to be served.

For example, the national parks in the United States were not created to be efficient; they were created to preserve price-less landscapes for the enjoyment of generations to come. This is a judgment about the public interest that does not involve efficiency. It makes sense to use resources available to the Na-tional Park Service efficiently, but suggesting this should be the primary value guiding park management is not the same thing as taking it into account as one value among several. Treating it as the primary value could result in decisions about wildlife and land and visitor management that contradict the public purposes of the parks. To illustrate, a direct route for a new park road might be more cost efficient than one that avoids sensitive wildlife habitat and selling space on park vehicles for corporate advertisements might provide a welcome boost to the park system budget. However, in this case as in others, efficiency is useful as an operational value but can be misplaced as a primary rationale for public action.

What Is Gained and What Is Lost: The Case of Vacation Beach

A fictional but realistic case study can illustrate the issue of making choices between efficiency and other values. City and county managers are career professionals, but they are also directly appointed by the governing body—the elected mayor and city council in a city, the board of commissioners or supervisors in a county—and they are at-will employees, which means the governing body may dismiss them at any time. City and county managers tend to be innovative advocates of professional management and, because they are accessible and accountable to elected officials and the taxpaying public, they often emphasize efficiency in their work.

The city manager of a tourist-oriented coastal city in Florida (we will call it Vacation Beach) decided to adopt features of NPM in city operations. Awareness of NPM-related concepts has spread throughout local government in the past two decades, so many elected officials expect managers they employ to apply these concepts to improve efficiency in their communities. Vacation Beach was experiencing financial pressure due to stagnant revenue and increasing costs for personnel and materials. Having heard members of the city council discuss the idea of "running government like a business," the city manager decided it was time for her staff to implement related ideas to show they were keeping up with important developments in the field. Accordingly, as a team, and working with the city council, the staff:

- increased the sales tax rate and hotel occupancy taxes to draw additional revenue from tourists;
- implemented performance measures wherever possible, quantifying items such as the number of customers served in the city utilities office, square feet of roadway repaved, vehicles worked on in the maintenance shop, citizens involved in a citizen participation program, building permits processed, and so on;
- adopted a pay-for-performance system in which employees received one-time bonuses based on their performance reviews, administered twice each year;
- used surveys to determine resident satisfaction with city services;
- adopted a flexible budget management system in which department heads could move funds between budget categories as needed instead of asking for approval by resolution from the city council;
- contracted out several positions in park maintenance and in engineering;
- contracted with a regional government for police dispatch services formerly part of the city police department;
- cut service hours for the city library, reduced the subsidy for the nonprofit community senior center, and reduced the number of summer recreation programs for children;
- added a staff position for the performance management system, including assisting with the employee bonus program and budgeting;
- added a public relations staff person to "sell" the city as an efficient, businesslike operation and handle inquiries from residents and the media; and
- put employees who regularly interact with the public through "customer service" training.

The city manager had kept up with professional and scholarly articles about the advantages and disadvantages of NPM techniques. For example, she knew that performance measures could require staff time to maintain, that focusing on measurable outcomes might result in insufficient attention to other city services that are not as easily tracked using quantitative measures, and that pay-for-performance systems were often seen as unfair by public employees. However, she assumed that being aware of these and other potential problems would help the staff prepare for them and take measures to offset them.

City staff periodically evaluated progress of the NPM program and made adjustments as needed. Now, two years later, the manager and a group of eight city staff were conducting a scheduled major assessment of the NPM program. The assistant city manager had been reading about public service values and suggested that the group include them in the assessment. They identified public service values that were positively affected, values that were negatively affected, and those that remained relatively unchanged.

The values that were positively affected were efficiency, customer service, responsiveness, transparency, innovativeness, and profitability. Because of cost-saving measures and contracting out some services that had been provided by city personnel (such as park maintenance), there had been modest decreases in overall expenditure which the staff interpreted as efficiencies. Customer service training seemed to improve how residents perceived their interactions with city staff, as shown in the surveys of satisfaction with city services; this was evidence of responsiveness. The annual budget was transformed by using performance measures and colorful explanatory graphics and by putting the entire budget online; this led to greater transparency. Encouraging city employees to propose better ways to do their work had resulted in some innovative new techniques. The staff was uncomfortable with the term "profitability," thinking it more relevant to the private sector; instead, they used the term "surplus." There were surpluses in both years of the program to date, in large part because of the increases in the sales and hotel occupancy taxes. Some of the surplus was consumed by the cost of the two additional staff positions.

The city manager and senior staff were aware of the potential negative effects of applying market techniques, so they were able to avoid some of them. NPM treats citizens like customers, focusing on pleasing them with efficient services and asking them what they think of the services they receive. This is different from the public service orientation of treating citizens as "owners" of the government, people who can be involved in self-governing by discussing and participating in decisions about public policies and programs. Vacation Beach has an active neighborhood organization system sponsored by the city, and citizen advisory committees for the budget, parks and recreation, the library, and other municipal functions, so the NPM program did not seem to negatively affect the public service value of participativeness.

The manager and staff found, though, that some other public service values appeared to have been negatively affected by the NPM program. These were accountability, fairness, pluralism, and social justice. Problems affecting accountability involved contracting out and budgeting. It proved difficult to be sure that people working in services that were contracted out were doing what they should be doing, and police managers did not think the regional dispatching service was very good compared to the in-house unit they had earlier. In the new flexible budgeting process, the city council was no longer involved in approving how funds were shifted from line item to line item within a departmental account. This made it easier for department heads to respond to unanticipated needs, which was more efficient than the old system, but council members were uneasy about some of the decisions that had been made. They had been heard discussing going back to the earlier system so that public money would be spent as elected officials intended.

The new employee bonus reward system, based on performance assessment, had a negative effect on the value fairness. Knowing in advance that systems that offered greater rewards to some employees than to others could be a source of discontent in a public organization, the senior staff took care to construct a valid performance measurement system and to offer modest rather than unusually large rewards for significant improvements in performance. Even so, a number of employees thought the performance measurement system too subjective and the rewards unfair to people who were important contributors but who were not recognized in the bonus system. It was also unclear whether the bonus system inspired people to work harder and smarter, or whether it simply gave bonuses to people who would have performed well anyway. The staff decided to reconsider the bonus system, and if they could not find good ways to address their concerns and to show measurable improvements in performance because of the rewards, they would recommend discontinuing the system.

Pluralism and social justice were affected by the NPM project because of budget cuts to the city library, the senior center, and summer recreation programs for children. These people-oriented services were believed to be inefficient because they did not directly contribute to basic needs such as public safety, infrastructure, and economic health, and they represented a transfer of wealth from some socioeconomic classes or age groups to others. However, the city manager's staff was uncomfortable with these impacts, which they thought might negatively affect the sense of community in their city.

The staff decided that three applicable public service values were largely unaffected by the project. These were public interest, representativeness; and participativeness. Participativeness was mentioned above. It was unaffected because there were a number of citizen participation activities in Vacation Beach that operated in parallel with the new focus on customer service. Along with the new surveys measuring residents' attitudes toward city services, the staff believed that these activities left representativeness (acting in accord with citizen preferences) largely unaffected or possibly somewhat improved.

In one area of the NPM project, performance measurement produced results that the staff found to be silly. One type of problem with performance measurement is that some public services do not lend themselves to quantification. The sense of community generated by a library, senior center, or summer recreation program is a good example. Another type of problem is measuring things that, as it turns out, should not be measured. In Vacation Beach, the number of staff meetings was measured in the first two years of the program. However, having more staff meetings does not necessarily mean people are being productive; there is a point at which more meetings are a waste of time or indicative of issues that should have been resolved earlier. The staff therefore decided to stop counting the number of meetings.

The setting of this fictional example is a local government in the United States, so the case study is not necessarily applicable to other levels of government or to the public sector in other countries. However, the reinventing government movement in the United States began in local government, and many of the related concepts have been widely adopted in cities and counties. The issues discussed by the Vacation Beach staff are not unusual, and they can be important to people in very different public agencies in other places.

The staff at Vacation Beach were aware of the disadvantages of NPM and its potential effects on public service values. They took measures to ameliorate some of the known negative effects and they periodically assessed progress to make corrections. Their summary evaluation was that it was worthwhile for the city to implement NPM because efficiency and, in some cases, effectiveness had increased. They also recognized the negatives: quantification of outcomes did not work well for some services; cost savings were largely offset by the costs of implementing the changes; the attempt to measure employee performance to increase efficiency was problematic; the flexible budgeting system was in trouble; contracting out created some management problems; and there were negative effects on social justice and sense of community.

It was agreed that staff would work to address these issues during the next year, looking for an improvement in the balance between efficiency-oriented values and other values that had been affected negatively by the NPM program. People came away from the experience of implementing an efficiency-based program with the lesson that greater attention to efficiency is helpful, but other public service values deserve attention as well.

VALUES ASSOCIATED WITH EFFICIENCY

Four public service values discussed in Chapter 2 are directly related to the market model of efficient public sector management: *profitability, innovativeness, responsiveness,* and *serviceability.* The meaning of profitability is straightforward. In *Reinventing Government,* Osborne and Gaebler (1993, chap. 7) urge public managers to find ways to earn profits instead of spending public money, such as charging user fees for services and selling products or services such as fertilizer from a sewage treatment plant and excess capacity in a prison that can be used by other jurisdictions. To give public managers an incentive to earn money instead of spending it, agency managers would be allowed to keep some or all of their profits to use on projects they think important, and financial incentives could be given to employees who earn money for their agency.

These activities are *entrepreneurial*, a value that does not appear in the research discussed in Chapter 2, but it is similar to innovativeness, exercising initiative to create something new. Whether an entrepreneurial public administration can be reconciled with the expectation that public organizations should be transparent, accountable, and accessible to citizen participation in policy making is open to question (Bellone and Goerl 1992; Terry 1993). In the American governmental system, the expectation is that public professionals will either follow the lead of elected officials or make policy recommendations to them for consideration. Acting alone without public discussion and legislative or executive approval could be regarded by leaders and citizens as inappropriate for the professional role. This leads to the conclusion that entrepreneurial initiative needs to be tempered with attention to the constitutional and legal context of the public sector. The nonprofit sector does not share this context, but in a particular organization the board of directors may expect to participate in decision making about major initiatives.

The public service values responsiveness (reflecting the preferences of elected leaders and citizens) and serviceability (providing quality service to the public and people in the organization) are part of "customer-driven government" in *Reinventing Government* (Osborne and Gaebler 1993, chap. 6). The idea is that by asking people what they want from the public sector (e.g., with a survey) and giving them efficient service, governments can show the sort of attention to pleasing customers that is found in the private sector. This idea assumes that staff members in traditional public agencies treat people in a mechanical, bureaucratic manner that is indifferent to the circumstances of the people they serve and that employees in a private firm are warm, welcoming, and efficient.

There are many examples today of public agencies that work to be customer-oriented, offering online services, schedules tailored to the needs of their clientele, and services shaped by feedback from their community of users. And, it must be said, not all customer interactions with the private sector are customer-friendly. Most people have had frustrating or upsetting experiences with employees of private companies who are not especially knowledgeable or helpful. Still, the point is well taken—it is a good thing for public organizations to pay attention to what the public would like them to do and how it wants them to do it.

The market model of public services, in which government is the producer and residents are consumers, works well for situations in which decisions have already been made about what services will be offered and, in general terms, how they will be done. Almost everyone would like the process of paying a tax or utility bill to be streamlined and efficient, just as most people would enjoy having local schools and libraries ask them what services should be prioritized and how service delivery could be improved. The potential disadvantage of focusing on the consumer approach is that in their relationship to government, people are more than consumers—they are citizens. Treating them only as consumers

> is a problem because government is not a business from which customers can voluntarily decide whether to purchase a product. It is, rather, a collective effort that includes every person within a defined geographic area (city, county, district, state, nation), and membership is involuntary unless a resident moves out of the jurisdiction. Mandatory membership carries with it a sense of the right to be involved if one so wishes in the process of deliberating and deciding on creation and implementation of public policy. . . . Customers, on the other hand, are people to be persuaded and sold an image, a product, or a service rather than people who deliberate and decide. (Box 1999, 35–36)

The issue here is preserving the right of citizens to govern in a democracy. Even a citizen who only participates in government by voting occasionally can choose to become more involved in deciding what government does by joining advocacy groups, participating in committees, task forces, and boards and commissions that advise elected leaders, or offering ideas and feedback on proposed actions by governments at all levels. Much as we find with other public service values, responsiveness and serviceability do not operate alone and out of context, but instead interact with other values such as representativeness and participativeness. Today, many public professionals take for granted the importance of being innovative and responsive. These values become part of the work of public service along with other values and they are integrated into a balanced view of the public service role in a constitutional democracy.

APPLYING EFFICIENCY IN PROFESSIONAL LIFE

We have found that the market perspective is pervasive in society and that the associated idea of economic efficiency has always been important in the public sector. This creates a tension between values for the public professional, because we assume that government—as an institution in society and as a complex set of organizations—is created to carry out public purposes more than to be efficient or to serve private interests.

Though public professionals do not rate efficiency or its related values high on a list of what is important to them, their daily work is shaped by the expectation of elected leaders and citizens that government should be run in a way that maximizes the use of resources and minimizes waste. In this sense efficiency is a "background value," always present as a consideration in designing programs and delivering services. Probably many public professionals, if asked, would say they assume their work should be efficient so they can get as much done as possible with the budgeted funds they have available.

Use of the market model of economic efficiency in the public sector becomes a problem when it disrupts values such as democracy, citizenship, self-governance, and social equity. Thinking of people as customers works well in managing systems in which residents pay bills, research public information, or purchase licenses; it does not work so well when it is time for citizens to discuss and decide issues of public policy. Efficiency and its associated values of entrepreneurial management can help with the micro-level, technical implementation of public services. It is less helpful in deciding at the macro level what services should be offered, how to fund them, and broadly how they should be structured. For this, values of democracy and citizenship are more useful and appropriate than economic values.

For the public professional, this means being aware of the trade-offs inherent in advising elected leaders and citizens about creating public policies and also in their implementation. There are times when efficiency is the prime value, more important than any other, and there are times when it is secondary, irrelevant, or even damaging. As the city manager and her staff discovered in Vacation Beach, implementing a set of management reforms grounded in efficiency involves trade-offs between values and also recognition that not everything governments and public professionals do is about minimizing cost.

In sum, we have found that the value of efficiency is, as expected, a very important part of managing in the public sector. It is also a value that public professionals need to apply carefully, knowing that government is about public purposes and that efficiency is one value among many in deciding about those purposes and putting them into practice. In this way we have answered the question posed in the introductory section of this chapter: "How can we bring together a personal commitment to the values of public service and the reality of the dominance of economic thought and action in society?" In the next chapter we turn to a classic, core value in public service, accountability. Whatever values are served by the choices political leaders make, public professionals may find themselves wondering whom they serve and for what purposes.

5

Accountability

Whom Do I Serve, and for What Purposes?

TYPES OF ACCOUNTABILITY

Accountability is about a relationship, one in which an individual, group, or organization must report to others, answer for performance, and be judged in relation to a concept or goal. Accountability is a common topic in books and articles on public affairs, which is not surprising, since it is an important part of exercising authority in a democracy. Public professionals may feel accountable to several types of stakeholders, including individual citizens, nonprofit organizations and private firms that interact with public agencies, people in the organizational hierarchy, elected leaders and their political appointees, and other professionals in the same occupational specialization. In addition to people or groups, public professionals may feel accountable to ideas, such as norms of professional practice (e.g., in law enforcement, planning, social work, or city management), guides to acceptable practice adopted by professional associations, or a personal sense of the public interest.

From Chapter 2, we have a definition of accountability used in a survey about public service values: "To act willingly in justifying and explaining one's actions to relevant stakeholders" (Molina and McKeown 2012, 380). It is interesting that this brief definition begins with the idea of willingness, which contrasts with an attitude of resistance to answering to others, or doing so grudgingly when pressed. A more detailed definition is given by Ronald Oakerson (1989, 114): "To be accountable means to have to answer for one's actions or inaction, and depending on the answer, to be exposed to potential sanctions, both positive and negative. Accountability can bring either blame and censure or recognition for a job well done."

Accountability can take several forms. Using the explosion of the space shuttle *Challenger* in 1986 as a way to compare and contrast forms of accountability, Barbara Romzek and Melvin Dubnick (1987) describe four types: *bureaucratic, legal, professional,* and *political.* According to Romzek and Dubnick, "The functioning of a *bureaucratic accountability* system involves two elements: an organized and legitimate relationship between a superior and a subordinate in which the need to follow 'orders' is unquestioned; and close supervision or a surrogate system of standard operating procedures or clearly stated rules and regulations" (228). This is the sort of accountability we think of in relation to organizational charts, job descriptions, and management techniques.

Legal accountability is the "relationship between a controlling party outside the agency and members of the organization." The controlling party consists of "the individual or group in a position to impose legal sanctions or assert formal contractual obligations"; these outsiders "make the laws and other policy mandates which the public administrator is obligated to enforce or implement" (228–229). This is the traditional structure of government in a representative democracy; the people elect their lawmakers and executives and career public professionals do as the lawmakers direct.

Romzek and Dubnick's third type, *professional accountability,* "is characterized by placement of control over organizational activities in the hands of the employee with the expertise or special skills to get the job done." In contrast to bureaucratic accountability, "under professional accountability the central relationship is similar to that found between a layperson and an expert, with the agency manager taking the role of the layperson and the workers making the important decisions that require their expertise" (229). Using the *Challenger* disaster to analyze accountability, Romzek and Dubnick argue that NASA's organizational environment exerts pressure to rely on "political, bureaucratic, and legal accountability mechanisms" (236) instead of giving sufficient weight to professional accountability, which is especially important given the sort of work NASA does.

The fourth type, *political accountability*, emphasizes responsiveness, in contrast to the deference given organizational employees in systems characterized by professional accountability. In this perspective, the "key relationship . . . resembles that between a representative (in this case, the public administrator) and his or her constituents (those to whom he or she is accountable). Under political accountability, the primary question becomes, 'Whom does the public administrator represent?' The potential constituencies include the general public, elected officials, agency heads, agency clientele, other special interest groups, and future generations" (229).

Much of what has been written about accountability in public affairs addresses ways that society can monitor and control public bureaucracies, which are often criticized as centers of waste and inefficiency. In recent years, with increasing reliance on contracting for services and cooperative efforts across organizations and sectors, the complex nature of accountability has become more evident. Public service can involve a networked or shared governance environment that includes nonprofit, private, and public organizations, elected leaders, citizens, and professional groups. In addition, the pressure of financial limitations and public skepticism about government accountability makes today's public service setting particularly challenging. As George Frederickson (1997, 175) puts it, "the perception that public bureaucracies are beyond control or unaccountable is widespread, although there is little evidence to support such a perception."

Given the complexity of the value of accountability, an individual public professional may feel accountable in several directions at once. This situation is not unlike the multiple sources of accountability in Romzek and Dubnick's political accountability, but the view of accountability used here addresses the bureaucratic, legal, and professional perspectives as well, to the extent that they apply in a specific situation. Along with the several sources of network accountability noted above, public professionals work in hierarchical organizations (bureaucratic accountability), many have commitments to norms of professional practice that shape their daily work (professional accountability), and they work in organizations that are led, ultimately, by elected officials (legal accountability).

Here, we approach accountability from the perspective of the individual public service professional, emphasizing the distinction between the professional role and the roles of elected leaders and political appointees. Dwight Waldo (1980, 107) writes of this distinction in the context of ethical decisions that public administrators make about whom they serve: "the ethical problems of a legislator are significantly different from those of a military officer, those of a regulatory commissioner different from those of a police chief." For career public service professionals, the question we want to explore takes into account the potential for multiple types of accountability: "Whom do I serve, and for what purposes?"

Some of the sections in this chapter parallel topics discussed in Chapter 3, addressing the Constitution and laws, organizations, and professional norms, but the focus is on how features of the administrative environment serve as sources of accountability for public professionals. In addition, the chapter is organized in a way that loosely follows Waldo's treatment (in *The Enterprise of Public Administration*) of "the *sources* and *types* of ethical obligations to which the public administrator is expected to respond" (Waldo 1980, 103). He outlines twelve types of ethical obligation: (1) the Constitution, (2) law, (3) nation or country, (4) democracy, (5) organizational-bureaucratic norms, (6) profession and professionalism, (7) family and friends, (8) self, (9) middle-range collectivities (party, class, race, interest group, etc.), (10) the public interest or general welfare, (11) humanity or the world, and (12) religion or God (103–106).

Ethics in public administration is more about choices people make in fulfilling their roles than about distinguishing right from wrong, so this emphasis on ethical obligations gives us a good start on an examination of the public service value of accountability. The rule of law is fundamental to describing the role of the public professional, so the next section discusses the public service value of lawfulness. This is followed by examination of several other sources of accountability and three associated values, *effectiveness, transparency,* and *duty.*

LAWFULNESS AS A KEY ELEMENT OF ACCOUNTABILITY

The public sector is built on a foundation of constitutionalism and rule of law. These structures of purpose and legality, which are the focus of many important issues in public service, are constantly changing, due to new legislation, decisions of the courts, and administrative regulations. It is not stretching the truth to say that the daily environment of public professionals consists of accountability to the system of governance created by the Constitution and the laws.

A national constitution is the ultimate source of accountability for people who work in public affairs, whether it is in written form or it is understood to be the cumulative result of tradition. As Sheila Kennedy and David Schultz (2011, 23) put it, "Understanding the philosophic roots of the US Constitution is critical to the enterprise of public management, because constitutions are the original declarations of, and frameworks for, public policy. They embody a society's most fundamental assumptions about law, legitimacy, and government power." This is a central element in accountability for public professionals, since "by definition, public management not rooted in the Constitution lacks legitimacy" (24). Authors such as Kennedy and Schulz, and John Rohr (1989), point to decisions of the courts as key tools to guide the actions of public administrators. David Rosenbloom, a scholar of law in public administration, writes:

> The U.S. Constitution is central to the organization and practice of public administration in this country. . . . During the second half of the twentieth century the federal courts, often led by the Supreme Court, vastly expanded individuals' constitutional rights in their encounters with public administration. Constitutional law became relevant, if not central, to administrative decisions and operations regarding clients and customers; public personnel systems; outsourcing; the treatment of patients in public mental health facilities; incarceration; and the exercise of regulatory authority in street-level encounters. . . . contemporary public administration is informed by and infused with constitutional concerns. (2003, 55–56)

The importance of the Constitution in creating a framework for the structure and functions of government is clear. However, this is a general framework, and the daily work of public management is largely shaped by more specific legal constraints. In addition, while the U.S. Constitution can be directly relevant to the work of public professionals in the national government, its applicability to those who work in state and local governments is less immediate. As we found in Chapter 1, there are 2.8 million federal civilian employees, 4.3 million state government employees, and 4.5 million local government employees not in education. Many federal employees do not often encounter issues that are directly related to the Constitution; this is likely to be especially true of state and local employees.

Even so, the governmental system created by the Constitution includes a wide range of legal, regulatory, and policy accountability for the daily work of people in public affairs. In a public professional's office we may find interpretations of the effects of state or federal court decisions, administrative regulations adopted following rule-making processes, a personnel handbook or collective bargaining agreement shaped by laws and negotiated contracts, the text of national or state laws or local ordinances, procedural manuals created according to legal guidelines, and legal contracts for services with nonprofit or private organizations. These things are evidence of managing according to various requirements that have a basis in law.

Managing an organization in a way that is accountable to all these features of the governmental system requires significant time and commitment. Across the range of public service occupations, we can find many in which practicing professionals know the importance of *lawfulness*, a key public service value in a democratic nation. This seemingly old-fashioned, basic value can be ignored in the rush to pay attention to the latest trends in management or current political or policy controversies. However, without attention to the constitutional and legal structure of society, nothing else is possible—lawfulness is a particularly important public service value and element of accountability.

ACCOUNTABILITY TO ELECTED LEADERS AND ORGANIZATIONAL SUPERIORS

Accountability to elected leaders and those in the organization who answer to them directly is the type most people have in mind when they want to know whether public professionals are doing what they should do. This type of accountability is linked to the classic, orthodox structure of a democratic republic in which responsibility is "owed upward, subordinate to superordinate, to the top of the pyramid, then bridged over by the electoral principle to the people." Authority, in contrast, moves in "the other direction, upward from the people through their elected representative, then bridged over the top of the pyramid and descending, echelon by echelon, to every officer and employee" (Waldo 1980, 110). In this "overhead democracy" structure (Redford 1969), the people do not directly determine how public services are delivered, nor do they supervise administration. Instead, they choose representatives who do this for them. According to Robert Behn (2001, 41),

> this concept of democratic accountability is clear, simple, and direct. Because government can separate administration from policy, and because the bureaucratic apparatus of government will find and adopt the most efficient way to implement any policy, the public need not worry about administration. Citizens need only to worry about the policy. And if they don't like their government's policies (or the way in which the legislature is overseeing the administration of these policies), citizens have a direct and effective means to correct the situation: They can vote their elected officials out of office. That is political accountability. That is direct accountability.

Behn suggests that this idea of accountability is influenced by the ideas of three important historical figures: Woodrow Wilson's nineteenth-century distinction between politics and administration, Frederick Winslow Taylor's early twentieth-century concepts of scientific management, and Max Weber's early twentieth-century model of bureaucracy as an efficient hierarchy. However, each of these ideas contains "fallacies" that call into question the idea of a simple democratic accountability. It is impossible to entirely separate politics from administration because implementing the law involves a host of choices about how it should be done, so that public service practitioners make daily workplace decisions that seem much like policy choices. Taylor sought the scientifically determined "one best way" to manage each work setting, but the reality of work in public affairs involves the potential for several ways to address the task at hand. And, while bureaucracy remains the primary model for organizational structure, today people often assume it will be slow, difficult to coordinate, and resistant to change (Behn 2001, 49–51).

So, instead of an autonomous professional service that waits for policy direction from elected leaders and carries it out without political interference, we have bureaucracies in need of oversight, monitoring, and correction. In addition to the problem of bureaucracies that are difficult to control, Hugh Miller and Charles Fox (2007) question the idea of representative democracy. Calling it the "representative democratic accountability feedback loop" (4), Miller and Fox noted that the loop model depends on citizens who know what they want, monitor public sector performance, and vote their preferences. The loop is ineffective, though, because "the wants and needs of the people are, by and large, manipulated" (7) by the commercial media, political candidates compete on image more than issues, many people do not vote, and politicians are influenced more by interest groups than by voters (8).

This critique seems to leave the orthodox view of professional accountability in public affairs in tatters: Miller and Fox characterize it as "dead" (2007, 3). If most citizens do not know what they want or have a distorted view of public affairs, if politicians are elected based on image rather than substance, and if elected leaders are influenced by interest groups rather than voters, we may legitimately ask why those leaders should be a primary focus of accountability for public professionals.

Miller and Fox (2007, chap. 2) identify several attempts to reform loop democracy, including the market approach of privatization and contracting out, a constitutional view of the role of public administration in a democracy that grants it a degree of legitimacy in representing the people, and a communitarian perspective emphasizing citizen involvement in public decision making. For Miller and Fox, none of these alternatives solves the problems of a misinformed, uninvolved citizenry, special interest influence, and the fragmentation of national, state, and local communities into many groups of people with different values and desires (chap. 3).

The orthodox overhead model of bureaucratic accountability does seem a bit out of date and frayed at the edges; using it requires us to add elaborations that take into account concerns expressed about its applicability in contemporary society. However, in the context of our examination of public service values, the orthodox view of structure and accountability in public affairs has an important advantage over the alternatives: it is the model that legislators, the courts, and most citizens who pay attention to government think is appropriate in the American system. Whatever the imperfections of the classic model of democracy and accountability, public service professionals have to work in the existing world of laws, organizations, and policy implementation.

In the daily work environment, while there can be several types of accountability, organizational superiors are responsible for hiring, discipline, and termination; they evaluate the work of public professionals; and they make decisions about their career advancement. Evaluation of the work of people in the organization is in part dependent on how well they have carried out the policy intent of elected officials. In this way, whatever the weaknesses of the classic model of accountability, it shapes the public service organization and the conduct of its staff.

However harsh or simplistic it may seem, for public professionals accountability unavoidably includes demonstrating that they have followed the policy leadership provided by the representative democracy structure. Other types of accountability—to citizens, the public interest, professional norms—are important, but it can be difficult for public professionals to remain in an organization if organizational superiors or elected leaders perceive them to be unaccountable, to be doing something other than what the leaders and superiors want done. In many situations, public professionals make complex decisions involving policy implementation, and they can be involved in policy creation as well. Their sense of service to the public can be broader than concern for accountability within the organizational hierarchy. Ultimately, though, as Kalu Kalu writes, "bureaucrats are essentially contractors in lieu of the public. They are not necessarily the initiators but rather the purveyors of the public mandate as may be captured in the constitutional (legitimate) authority of the government under which they operate" (Kalu 2003, 541). This basic characteristic of public affairs places elected leaders and organizational superiors at the forefront of the value of accountability.

ACCOUNTABILITY TO CITIZENS

It seems natural in a democracy for those who do the work of the public to interact with the people themselves, using the knowledge they gain to shape service delivery. However, a direct connection between unelected public employees and the preferences of citizens was not intended in the founding design of the American government. Even today, when public professionals work directly with citizens, political leaders expect them to be accountable in following policy direction rather than public opinion. Political leaders do not expect professionals to interact with the public in a way that would influence what citizens think about public policies and services.

In the Chapter 3 section on challenges to neutrality, it was noted that public professionals have on-the-ground knowledge of conditions that political leaders are not likely to have, in addition to their knowledge of the technical details of service delivery. Though the representative, or loop, model of institutional structure would reserve interaction with the public to elected leaders, the realities of daily public service make this impractical and unrealistic.

Many people who work in public organizations rarely if ever interact with the public or do so only in simple transactional settings (such as payment of a water bill or renewal of a driver's license), but there are others whose exposure to social conditions and public issues gives them valuable perspective on policies and methods of service delivery. Examples include the manager of an Internal Revenue Service center that handles questions from taxpayers, a state inspector who evaluates the safety of nursing homes, a city planner who works with neighborhood groups, and a police captain who supervises a street patrol unit in a central city. Each of these people is in a good position to understand how adopted laws and policies are functioning in daily application and to make recommendations that would improve outcomes.

These public professionals may feel a sense of accountability to citizens because they know how policies or practices could be changed in order to improve public services. This form of accountability can be especially significant when citizen involvement in governance is central to the work being done. In many places nationwide, state and local governments have created programs that bring citizens directly into the policy-making process, providing them with information and staff support, and putting them in the position of making recommendations that are taken seriously in decision making. These programs run counter to contemporary citizen apathy, disengagement, and dislike of public affairs. Though they involve only a fraction of the population, they show the value of democracy and participativeness in helping to build community cohesiveness and address issues that government cannot easily solve on its own (Thomas 2012, chap. 7).

Examples of effective citizen involvement opportunities include making recommendations on local land-use plans and proposals; planning for community features such as bike paths, public parks, and infrastructure; providing input on budgeting priorities; and assessing social service needs. Public organizations can use citizen involvement to inform the public of proposed actions or to gather information or preferences from citizens, they may collaborate with citizens in settings where the "agency retains decision power, but is strongly influenced by the products of the process," or they may delegate decision making to the public (Timney 2011, 93).

There are well-known difficulties and limitations associated with citizen involvement in governance (Thomas 2012, chap. 7). Apathy and disinterest are an ongoing problem, though where programs address issues people care about and give them meaningful opportunities to create change, it can be surprising how many people want to participate. Resources are another potential problem area. To be successful, most citizen involvement efforts need staff support, which can be hard to supply in a time of fiscal pressure on the public sector.

Often, we think of "the public" as monolithic, a body of people with similar preferences for public action. Instead, in many citizen involvement settings we find a wide range of views on current conditions and ideas about what should be done. For the professional staff member, this situation requires respect for multiple perspectives and willingness to take the time needed to work through differences and reach solutions that most participants find acceptable.

Another potential source of complexity is the influence of groups and individuals external to the dialogue of the involvement process, including the elected governing body, business leaders, property owners, and groups with specific, defined agendas or policy preferences. Here is an example from the author's personal experience as a planner working with citizens in creating a comprehensive city plan in a medium-sized community in Oregon. The citizen's group had studied provisions of state law requiring attention to growth management (today this is often referred to as "smart growth"). Together, we took our preliminary concepts to the city planning commission for review. The planning commission made some suggestions, but largely supported what we were doing.

People from the business community had attended the planning commission meeting but did not comment on the preliminary plan. However, when the plan and the planning commission's recommendation were scheduled for discussion by the governing body (the city council), leaders of the Chamber of Commerce expressed their displeasure to the mayor and members of the council. They had waited to comment until the plan was ready for discussion by elected officials who would be more responsive to their views than would members of the planning commission. Presumably they thought the commission would be focused on planning concepts, while council members would be thinking about media coverage and public reaction.

Several members of the citizen's group felt betrayed. They had invested time and energy in the plan, and the local businesspeople who were criticizing it had chosen not to participate in the planning process, either as committee members or in discussion with the planning commission. Instead, they waited to object to it at the level of final review by elected officials. The outcome was not as bad as it seemed it might be; the city council's review of the plan was delayed until Chamber of Commerce representatives could review it more thoroughly, a few policy and mapping changes were made, and eventually the plan was approved. For our discussion of accountability as a public service value, the point is that several demands for accountability can be felt at the same time, and the perspectives of those asking the public professional for accountability can be in conflict.

PROFESSIONAL ACCOUNTABILITY

The discussion of professional values in Chapter 3 treats them as constraints that help define the practitioner's role. In this section we want to consider the professional role from the perspective of sources of accountability—that is, people, groups, and ideas that public professionals think are important in their work. When we use the term "professional role," we mean those workplace behaviors that coworkers, organization leaders, professional peers, and the public expect from people filling similar positions (e.g., a children's services case worker, wildlife biologist).

Public service professions are defined by the tasks expected of people who work in them, as well as by expectations for how those people interact with others. We see these expectations in announcements for open positions, in job descriptions, and in the behaviors of public professionals. We expect, for example, a manager in the U.S. Forest Service to have particular duties, to speak with the public in certain ways about issues of interest in the management of federal lands, and to interact in certain ways with agency staff, people from other organizations, and elected officials. When a person acts as we expect, we believe she or he is filling the professional role appropriately; if the same person acts somehow unexpectedly, we may wonder whether we have understood the role incorrectly or if this person's behavior is different from that of most people who fill the role.

The idea of role conflict is a useful way to think about professional accountability. It occurs when someone feels pulled in different directions simultaneously, so that being accountable to a particular person, group, or idea will make being accountable to others more difficult. Terry Cooper (2012, 112) ties this perspective on accountability to ethics, stressing the importance of resolving role conflicts: "Orders, edicts, rewards, human relations training, and organizational development strategies are not likely to accomplish much if we do not encourage and systematically develop responsibility by addressing ethical dilemmas that arise from role conflicts."

In *The Responsible Administrator*, Cooper relates a fictional case study about the public health officer (PHO) for the City of Micro, a second-level person in the municipal health department. The work of the department "involves inspecting restaurants, food markets, food-processing plants, and sanitary facilities for large public buildings" (Cooper 2012, 99).

Micro is experiencing financial pressure, embodied in recent budget cuts. Members of the city council think that a rock concert might produce significant revenue for the city, so they approve a contract with a concert promoter named Ripley. In developing plans for the concert, Ripley estimates that half a million people will attend the event for fourteen hours. However, people will be gathering for days in advance, so public services will be required for several days.

It happens that in this case there are no adopted, applicable state or local legal requirements for public facilities at events such as this. The PHO suggests using a recommendation created some time ago by the National Public Health Association (NPHA), a nonprofit professional organization in which the PHO is an active member and leader. This recommendation calls for one portable toilet for each fifty concert attendees, which in this case would be 10,000 toilets at the proposed concert. This is a very large number of toilets, which could make costs prohibitive and reduce space available for attendees. Ripley, the concert promoter, counters with a proposal for one toilet for every 300 people. He also reacts negatively to the PHO's ideas about medical tents and personnel, the amount of food, and trucks of water, saying he will go to the city council to complain about the requirements.

Later on, Harley, the director of Micro's health department, asks the PHO to be reasonable. This request follows a phone call Harley received from the president of the city council. Harley reminds the PHO that there are no legal requirements, it is a one-day event, and there is public support for the concert among citizens of Micro. The PHO is now in a difficult situation, one that highlights accountability to professional standards, to the city council, to the director of the department, to the department itself, to the interests of the citizens of Micro, and to the safety of concert attendees.

Accountability to the professional organization, the NPHA, is significant. The PHO is a long-time member, a leader in advocating high standards in public health, and a member of the committee that developed the standards Ripley is resisting. As Cooper describes the PHO's sense of accountability to the NPHA, "you are particularly concerned about how you will be perceived by the members of the NPHA. Your professional integrity is at stake" (Cooper 2012, 102).

Accountability to the municipal health department and its director is important as well. The director, Harley, who has been supportive of the PHO in other situations, has integrity, good judgment, and a sense of proportion. The reputation of the department and its standing with the city council could be damaged by taking an unpopular position. The PHO certainly feels a responsibility to support the director and the people and work of the department.

The PHO is clearly accountable to the city council, which has ultimate authority and responsibility for decisions made in the name of the city. If the PHO stands firm with the NPHA's recommendation, the council could hold an open hearing on the matter and inflame the public. The PHO might be fired or put into a dead-end job and could become "the butt of a joke about ten thousand toilets" (Cooper 2012, 102). It might be possible to negotiate a compromise with Ripley to resolve the situation, but if the PHO is "discredited or fired, the council will probably give Ripley a free rein to do as he pleases" (102).

There is also, of course, the problem of potential consequences if the PHO gives Ripley what he wants and there is an outbreak of disease or an accident or disturbance requiring medical care for a large number of people. This consideration reflects professional accountability to the safety of concertgoers and to the citizens of Micro because of potential liability.

Some public professionals are infrequently, or never, presented with circumstances like this one, in which accountability pulls them in several directions at once. Even so, this is not an uncommon sort of situation in public service, which can produce difficult and challenging role conflicts that strain the public professional's ability to accommodate multiple demands for accountability. In the Micro case, Cooper (2012, 110–111) outlines an option that allows flexibility in negotiating standards for the concert, along with asking the city council to phase in new requirements over a period of time. This compromise solves the current problem and preserves the PHO's reputation for supporting strong standards.

This case study brings to mind the question from earlier in the chapter, "Whom do I serve, and for what purposes?" Does the PHO serve the rationality of a professional organization and its recommendation (which, it seems now, could have been somewhat out of touch with actual conditions present at large events such as the concert), or organizational demands for accountability (the financial condition of the city, the future of the department, relationship with the director), or the public interest (liability, safety), or personal status and career (the possibility of losing effectiveness or being fired)? If the answer is "yes," meaning all of these forms of accountability must be considered at once, how are they to be prioritized? As we might expect, the Micro case illustrates the potential complexity of professional accountability when there is no quick or easy answer to this question.

THE PUBLIC INTEREST AS A SOURCE OF ACCOUNTABILITY

The public interest as a public service value is examined further in Chapter 7, but something can be said about it as well in the context of accountability. Discussion of the idea of public interest often involves broad concepts such as climate change, the future of a community, or the welfare of future generations. In the daily management of public organizations, though, the public interest is more often connected to specific issues. For example, in an agency that monitors water quality, the public interest for technical staff could be keeping drinking water free of contaminants that harm customers. For a state transportation engineer, the public interest might be providing efficient transport between major cities. For a community involvement specialist, the public interest could be maximizing opportunities for citizens to participate in decision making about community issues. In these settings and many others, the public interest that concerns practitioners is specifically related to the purpose of their work and the goals of their organizations.

Micro's health officer was thinking about the public interest in considering possible impacts on residents of the community and on people who would come to the proposed concert. Public professionals may think of themselves as accountable to a public interest that is more compelling than the current preferences of elected leaders or organizational superiors. This can lead to role conflict in which the professional must choose whether to act on this perception of the public interest or, instead, to avoid the risks involved by complying with adopted policy. A choice to act on one's view of the public interest may not rise to the level of causing a problem in the organization, or it might result in a response by superiors or elected leaders that could endanger the practitioner's position.

In the Micro case, any actions taken would be visible to the people involved. In some situations, though, when public professionals view the public interest differently from others in their organization, they may "work against the wishes—either implicitly or explicitly communicated—of their superiors" behind the scenes. This "is a form of dissent carried out by those who are dissatisfied with the actions of public organizations, programs, or people but who typically choose strategically not to go public with their concerns in whole or in part" (O'Leary 2006, xi).

These people might stretch the limits of existing rules or policies, such as an environmental enforcement manager who pursues violators with more energy and determination than expected, or a social services case manager who grants exceptions or special benefits to clients on humanitarian grounds despite policies that discourage doing so. Others might gather information and shape professional reports in ways that weaken existing policies or practices, encouraging changes that advance a particular vision of the public interest. Some of these people might leak information to select groups or individuals outside their organizations who can use it to counter, resist, or change policies or laws. They might work directly with outside groups, helping them develop action plans in pursuit of their goals.

Though it is relatively uncommon, if the conflict between accountability to the organization and accountability to the public interest becomes acute, public professionals may feel that their sense of self and integrity is threatened. This might happen if it seems clear that the organization is violating laws, there is gross mismanagement, or organizational policies will do damage to people or the environment. Public professionals may then wonder whether it is possible to "live with ourselves if we comply with certain orders or fail to oppose particular decisions or activities." In such cases, "our ultimate obligation to the public may call for actions that breach our loyalty to the organizational hierarchy—in other words, whistleblowing" (Cooper 2012, 236, 198).

Though whistleblowing may occur within an organization, in common usage it means giving up on change within the organization and taking one's message outside. This is not done by quietly leaking information or working with outside groups, but by making a disagreement with policy or a claim about organizational wrongdoing publicly known. Despite national and state laws that offer some protections to whistleblowers, this is a very serious step to take. People in the organizational hierarchy will have trouble trusting the whistleblower in the future, and the whistleblower's career in a particular organization may be effectively at an end, even if the person remains employed there. Retaliatory actions against whistleblowers can be significant, such as focusing on whistleblowers instead of the issues they raise; manufacturing poor work records for whistleblowers; threatening, isolating, humiliating, or prosecuting them; or eliminating their jobs (Svara 2015, 149–150).

Working covertly against the policies or preferences of organization superiors or elected leaders, and especially whistleblowing, are actions taken outside of accountability to the organization. They show accountability to the public interest or to some other source of accountability instead of the organization. While in the Micro case the public interest is one of several sources of accountability competing for attention, for a public professional to set aside organizational accountability in favor of the public interest is a matter of some weight and importance.

VALUES ASSOCIATED WITH ACCOUNTABILITY

Several of the values identified in Chapter 2 as important to public professionals are associated with accountability, including dedication, reliability, respect, responsiveness, lawfulness, organizational interest, effectiveness, and transparency. *Lawfulness* and *organizational interest* are discussed above. *Effectiveness* and *transparency* are especially relevant to the discussion in this chapter. In addition, *duty* may be added as another way of thinking about accountability.

Effectiveness has always been a basic value in public administration along with efficiency. It can be argued that effectiveness is of primary importance and that efficiency, while important, is not essential to effective service delivery. A service that is effective but inefficient is doing what it is supposed to do, though its cost needs attention. A service that is economically efficient but in some ways ineffective, in contrast, fails to fulfill its legislative mandate. Because the objective is to deliver services that do what is expected, doing the wrong thing, or the right thing in the wrong way, is ultimately inefficient.

What we mean by effectiveness can be complicated, and it may be determined in a number of ways, singly or in combination. Among other possibilities, effectiveness might be determined by measurement using performance metrics or benchmarking, by the impressions people have of interpersonal or teamwork skills, by a program's ability to stay within its budget, by the perceptions of elected leaders about service effectiveness, and by surveys of citizen satisfaction with public services. Whatever people mean when they use the term "effectiveness" in a particular situation, clearly it is a core public service value. Without effectiveness, many other public service values lose some of their meaning, and whatever view one holds about values such as efficiency, integrity, or the public interest, most people will agree that effectiveness is of primary importance.

Transparency, an important part of the idea of democracy, is closely related to accountability. Carolyn Ball (2009, 293) describes it as having three possible meanings: (1) "a public value embraced by society to counter corruption"; (2) "open decision-making by governments and nonprofits"; and (3) "a complex tool of good governance in programs, policies, organizations, and nations." At the level of individual action, transparency can be defined as "fulfilling one's duties in a manner that is open and visible" (Molina and McKeown 2012, 380).

If there are periodic revelations about corruption in a public organization, if there seems to have been tampering with the election process, if citizens have to insist before public officials will release information, or if laws are made and decisions taken in secrecy, people will worry about transparency. This worry is a stand-in for concern about whether the connection between citizens and their government is being strained, or whether certain groups or individuals have too much control over systems and procedures that should be open to public scrutiny and change.

We know that not everything can be done in the open. There are obvious examples such as personnel files, discussion of pending litigation, sensitive matters of national security, and certain categories of executive communication. Beyond that, however, we expect the public sector to operate in the open; we assume that secrecy and democracy are generally opposed to each other. This is somewhat ironic, since the U.S. Constitution was created in a secret process: James Madison's notes, the primary record of the Constitutional Convention, were not released until fifty years later. Today, websites for all levels of government give access to information about laws, administrative departments, ongoing projects and programs, and political and administrative decisions. Even with this flood of information, many events and issues involving governmental secrecy or suppression of embarrassing information come to public attention—enough to make many citizens skeptical about how transparent government is or intends to be.

Such incidents do not weaken our expectation that the public sector should be as transparent as possible. We know that large, remote federal agencies may be relatively opaque instead of transparent, so our negative reactions to lack of transparency are mostly limited to especially unpleasant revelations about their behavior. At the local level, because the scale of systems is smaller and the people who govern and run public organizations are closer to us, our expectations for transparency can be higher and more demanding. The case study of Micro is an example; the PHO felt accountable in an immediate, personal way because of physical proximity to the people involved and because the responsibility for making a decision was uniquely individual. In short, the PHO was right there, everyone was watching, and a decision had to be made—this is quite a sense of accountability.

James Svara (2015, 12–13) acknowledges that "duty is an old-fashioned term," one that "implies obligations, responsibilities, and meeting expectations." However old-fashioned it may be, it is clearly related to accountability, and it is not unusual for public professionals to think of their obligations as duties. Svara's discussion of duty, like accountability, is about the role of the public professional, specifically, "the behaviors expected of persons who occupy certain roles; that is, the obligations taken on when assuming a role or profession" (12). Career work in public affairs carries with it a sense of obligation, of duty. However much we make accountability a matter of analysis of connections between practitioners and others, the foundational concept for public professionals is that "duty has a special importance. They must serve the public, fulfill the expectations of public office, and be trustees of public resources" (Svara 2015, 12). Though duty does not appear in the research discussed in Chapter 2, it captures a sense of the nature of work in public affairs that adds meaning to the public service value of accountability.

APPLYING ACCOUNTABILITY IN PROFESSIONAL LIFE

We have examined the concept of accountability by identifying some of its sources for the public professional: lawfulness, elected leaders and organizational superiors, citizens, professional norms, the public interest, and the values of effectiveness, transparency, and duty. These values and sources of accountability are more than constraints on the behavior of public professionals or ways to describe the boundaries of the professional role. They define the nature of public service in a democracy, the reasons for a professional public service, and its relationship to citizens and the broader public interest.

It is apparent that accountability is a complicated matter in an era of public dissatisfaction with government and the complexity created by networked governance, with its blurred boundaries and uncertain lines of authority. Discussing accountability only as a constraint gives it a restrictive, limiting feeling that is not entirely appropriate. Accountability is not only about doing what is expected or suffering the consequences; it is also about accepting that public service involves responsibility, or duty, to an ideal of democratic governance. This ideal goes beyond the details of measurement, efficiency, or performance; it reflects the question "Whom do I serve, and for what purposes?"

This question may be overlooked during the daily rush of tasks to be done and problems to be solved, but as the health officer in Micro found, it can have immediate, significant meaning for someone faced with a difficult decision. Accountability proves to be useful in sorting out one's obligations in the work setting, connecting important, broad ideas about democracy and public service with the facts of problems to be solved, decisions to be made, and services to be delivered. Janet and Robert Denhardt (2011, 134) put this point well: "The complexity of public accountability faced by public servants is recognized as a challenge, an opportunity, and a calling. It requires expertise, a commitment to democratic ideals, knowledge of public law, and judgment formed by experience."

6

Public Service

The Personal Commitment

CORE ELEMENTS OF PUBLIC SERVICE

For many people, working in a public or nonprofit sector organization is much like working in any organization. There are satisfactions from a job well done, recognition and rewards, and a paycheck and benefits. For some others, though, there is something different, something important, about working for the public, whether in a government agency or in a nonprofit organization that serves a broad public interest. These people may have chosen to work in a public or nonprofit organization because of this difference, or they may have discovered it later on, when they had gained some experience in public service.

There is more than one way that people think about their reasons for valuing public service. According to James Perry and Lois Recascino Wise (1990, 368), "public service motivation may be understood as an individual's predisposition to respond to motives grounded primarily or uniquely in public institutions and organizations." Drawing from the work of several authors, Perry and Wise (1990) suggest that this predisposition may include any of a number of specific motivational elements, such as participating in policy formulation, commitment to a particular program, advocacy for a specific interest, a desire to serve the public interest, loyalty to duty and the government, social equity, and a "patriotism of benevolence" consisting of a desire to protect the rights of the people.

In a later article, Perry and Wise, with Annie Hondeghem (2010), review definitions of public service motivation from additional authors, concluding that in a general sense "it is a particular form of altruism or prosocial motivation that is animated by specific dispositions and values arising from public institutions and missions" (682). They write that public service motivations are found in both the public and nonprofit sectors, especially given the current "blurring of boundaries between sectors" (682), but they are often found in government because of the connection to providing public services. A person's reasons for finding public service attractive are not fixed or unchangeable, as Perry and Wise (1990, 369) note:

> Of course, people are a mix of motives, exhibiting combinations of values over a lifetime and focusing on different motives at various points in their careers. Personal or environmental factors might account for changes in individual motives, but clearly an individual can switch among public service motives as well as away from these stimuli altogether.

The next chapter, Chapter 7, examines the meaning of public interest, especially the process of identifying and acting on a specific policy option among competing possibilities. In this chapter, we explore the commitment of individual public professionals to public service, in particular the values they might find most influential in their work. We can think of the public interest as an "external" concept involving many people, a community, or society as a whole. The public service values held by individuals, in contrast, are "internal" concepts that may affect how each person approaches her or his work.

In Chapter 2 we found there are many values public service professionals care about. Which of these to address in a chapter on public service as a personal commitment is a difficult choice to make, but my experiences as a teacher and practitioner suggest that two things are of particular importance to many public service professionals. The first of these is integrity, a term drawn from the Latin word "integer," meaning whole, complete, entire; online definitions of integrity include words such as "unimpaired," "honest," "incorruptible," and "of sound moral character." Integrity is a broad idea that can be used in several different ways, applying to things as well as people (e.g., "the integrity of the ecosystem") and to practices as well as behavior (e.g., "artistic integrity").

For our purposes in exploring values in professional public service, we can think of integrity as carrying out one's duty in a manner consistent with one's values. This view of service and duty is related to the values of neutrality, loyalty, honesty, and accountability (honesty and integrity are sometimes found together, as in "she acted with honesty and integrity"), but it also carries with it an expectation of resistance to external influences that a professional believes to be inappropriate.

The second thing of importance to public professionals emphasized here is not a single value, but the idea of "making a difference." As noted above, not everyone finds unique satisfactions from public service, but some who do express a view of their role that connects with values such as social justice, inclusiveness, compassion, innovativeness, effectiveness, and participativeness. Their inspiration for working in public service is the opportunity to make something about the world better—this is an altruistic perspective that focuses attention on the good of others rather than self-interest.

The sections below explore the environmental context of professional public service, professional integrity, and the concept of public professionals as agents of change. Professional integrity is examined through a case study of a local planner faced with an awkward conflict in values. The concluding sections examine the value of empathy and use a case study of the branch manager of a state social services agency to illustrate application of the public service values discussed in the chapter.

THE ENVIRONMENT OF PROFESSIONAL PUBLIC SERVICE

The societal environment of public service has always been challenging; as noted in Chapter 1, politics and economics can significantly affect the work of public professionals. Though many public professionals are relatively insulated or removed from the disturbances caused by negative attitudes toward government, political transitions, changes in public opinion, reorganizations, cutbacks, and other sources of uncertainty and stress, many others are directly affected by events in the environment. In recent years, the political and economic environment has been especially difficult, with political polarization and financial uncertainty at the national level and fiscal retrenchment in many state and local governments. Impacts on jobs and conditions of employment in the public sector have been substantial, and conditions may be unsettled for some time to come.

This should not be too surprising. In a society where the purposes and legitimacy of government are often in question, we can expect the context of public service to cause turbulence that requires creative responses and adaptation. There is always tension between the value of democracy and the characteristics of government, which is often more effective and efficient than it is participative and transparent. As Mary Hamilton (2014, 275) put it, "That public service in a democracy is a paradox has been and continues to be a central issue in public administration." In this paradoxical setting, "public service and democracy are antithetical yet complementary" (286). They are antithetical because a professional public service seems undemocratic and complementary because the existence of democracy depends on a strong and competent public service.

This situation—the need for a strong public service in a country ambivalent about government—can be thought of as a glass half empty or a glass half full. The pessimists among us may find the challenging environment of public service frustrating and disappointing, while the optimists may think of it as an opportunity for new and interesting experiences. For our discussion, the question is what effects the environment can have on public service values. When hot political issues, the wishes of individual elected leaders, or the agendas of interest groups intrude on daily practice, what becomes of values such as neutrality, accountability, efficiency, honesty, transparency, the public interest, and so on?

In Chapter 4, we discussed the idea of long-term swings in national politics and economics. At one end of a continuum are times when private interest seems most important—relatively free markets, an emphasis on money and personal benefit—and at the other end are times when people focus on public purpose, using government to address problems in the social and physical worlds. This idea of long-term swings describes an important part of the environment of public affairs. Other features of this environment that can also influence public service are human behavior, economic inequality, role differences between the public and nonprofit sectors, and the effects of a specific organizational setting.

Human Behavior

The Federalist Papers are a collection of eighty-five essays that were published in newspapers in 1787 and 1788, written primarily by James Madison and Alexander Hamilton, with five written by John Jay. The purpose of the *Papers* was to explain and justify the design of the newly drafted Constitution and to convince the public that it should be adopted. Today, they provide insight into the thought of the people who wrote the Constitution, including ideas on the structure of the national government and relationships between its parts, the relationship between the national and state governments, and many other issues central to the American system of government.

The authors portray human beings as sometimes altruistic or public-regarding, but often as self-serving and seeking to centralize power for their own purposes. What Madison and Hamilton had to say about human behavior is not insignificant, since the structure of the new government was formed in large part in response to their beliefs about how people behave when they hold positions of power. Because they were worried that people would gather too much power and abuse others, the founders of the Constitution created a system that split authority between branches of government and between the states and the national government. *Federalist No. 51*, which is often used to highlight the founders' view of human behavior, can be summarized as follows:

> The language used to describe human nature makes this *Paper* notable. In the fourth paragraph, Madison writes that each part of the proposed

government should be given the means to defend itself from attack by the others, with the government structured in the Constitution so that "ambition must be made to counteract ambition." Thus, people are portrayed as power-hungry and aggressive, a view for which Madison makes no apology. Instead, acknowledging the meaning of the proposed form of government for the way people behave, he writes that "If men were angels, no government would be necessary," and that once a government is created to control the governed, then it is necessary to "oblige it to control itself." (Box 2014, 43)

Madison assumed that people who serve in government will bring with them their personal desires for power, so the structure of government must be used to limit and control their impulses. Human history contains many examples of behavior we could characterize as self-interested, greedy, and power-hungry. Though Madison and Hamilton were writing more than two centuries ago, we see much the same behavior today. Philosopher Richard Rorty (1999, 206) puts it this way:

> To say that history is "the history of class struggle" is still true, if it is interpreted to mean that in every culture, under every form of government, and in every imaginable situation . . . the people who have already got their hands on money and power will lie, cheat and steal in order to make sure that they and their descendants monopolize both forever.

This may seem overstated, but think of what is happening today. A variety of authors and sources could be cited on the condition of the world and the role of human behavior in shaping it, but we are already aware because we are surrounded by around-the-clock information and images. Every day, media coverage is more than enough to make the point: risky and fraudulent investment schemes that cost the public huge sums; corporate and special interest lobbying that shapes legislation, distorts representation, and weakens regulation; political campaigns funded by the wealth of billionaires; administrative decision making influenced by political and economic elites; tragic and awful violence and wars; discrimination and cruelty grounded in gender, race, religious difference, or national origin; and so on.

There is, of course, a community-oriented, benevolent side to human behavior evident in many organizations, civic activities, government programs, and individual acts of kindness. For those who work in public affairs, though, realistic knowledge of how people behave, what motivates them, and how public and non-profit organizations have been and can be used for private benefit is very useful for successful professional practice.

Social Inequality

It has become common to hear discussions about inequalities of wealth and power. Nevertheless, many people want to believe they live in a relatively equal society, not terribly unequal in economic circumstances, and as equal as possible in opportunities for people to better themselves through personal effort. Expressing concern openly about poverty, lack of social mobility, and concentrations of wealth so great that a small percentage of the population owns a large percentage of the wealth can lead to being labeled a socialist or someone engaged in "class warfare."

Today, concentration of wealth and the influence of money on the political process make it difficult to avoid thinking about the extent to which great inequality is compatible with democracy, and whether it is sustainable. As discussed in the section on private interest and public purpose in Chapter 4, economic inequality in the contemporary United States is approaching the levels experienced during the Gilded Age of the 1890s. In an article examining the wealth and income of the "top 1 percent" of the population, Alvaredo et al. (2013, 16) show that the income share of the top 1 percent in the United States has more than doubled in the past thirty years and that wealth concentration at the top of the socioeconomic scale is considerably greater in the United States than in other countries.

People in the United States are often thought to favor a society in which the free market allows the wealthy to become as wealthy as they like. However, Americans are not fully aware of the extent of the growing concentration of wealth in the United States, and they actually prefer a much more equal society. Michael Norton and Dan Ariely conducted a random-sample survey of 5,522 people in 2005 to discover what Americans think of the current and the ideal distribution of wealth. Survey respondents believed that the current distribution is much more equal than it actually is, and they preferred a distribution even more equal than that. Respondents thought the top 20 percent own 59 percent of the nation's wealth and should own 32 percent. However, they actually own 84 percent of the wealth. The wealth distribution preferred by 92 percent of this sample of Americans is more like that of contemporary Sweden than that of the United States (Norton and Ariely 2011). This is interesting, since Sweden is often negatively characterized in the United States as socialist. This is a large random sample, so we are relatively safe in assuming it reflects public opinion on this issue.

Though inequality is growing rapidly and has reached levels not seen for many decades, it may not be a serious problem if people are able to move up in the income and wealth distribution because of their own efforts. This is the "American dream" and many people think it is especially true in the United States. However, at the same time that inequality has become more pronounced in the United States than in most other developed nations, economic mobility has not increased. Today, American society presents fewer opportunities for advancement than are found in most other developed nations.

Researchers measure these opportunities using the concept of "intergenerational social mobility." In a report documenting this phenomenon across several developed countries, the Organisation for Economic Co-operation and Development found that social mobility is considerably lower in the United Kingdom, Italy, the United States, and France than it is in Canada, Australia, Denmark, Norway, Sweden, and Finland (OECD 2010).

The countries in the latter group have more fully developed systems for the education and support of children, families, and people in need than does the United States. Contrary to a common assumption that social mobility is largely or entirely a matter of individual effort and that it is hampered by public sector involvement, it appears that people in these countries benefit from a combination of high social mobility and governmental efforts supporting social development. Though we may not be sure to what extent these governmental efforts contribute directly to intergenerational mobility, they do not appear to damage it.

The implications of growing economic inequality and relatively low social mobility are potentially significant for public affairs and public service values. Values such as benevolence, compassion, and social equity are clearly directly connected with this issue. A number of other values, such as neutrality, efficiency, expertise, loyalty, democracy, and the public interest, may also be involved in professional settings where people are dealing with the effects of inequality and low mobility. To the extent that difficult social conditions make for contentious public discussion on policy options, public professionals may find their value priorities tested in practice.

Role Differences Between the Public and Nonprofit Sectors

There is a tendency to think of management as much the same in each sector—private, public, and nonprofit. Of course there are similarities, and in recent decades private sector management concepts have been especially prominent in the public sector. Nevertheless, it is not true that management is the same across sectors, in large part because of the specific constraints, legal requirements, and public attitudes toward the roles that people should play in each sector.

Our discussion is focused on the public sector, but many professionals in the nonprofit sector are also interested in public service values. This interest may not be found in equal measure across the entire sector, which includes organizations created to manage or advocate for specific group interests rather than the broader public interest. Examples include professional associations (e.g., physicians, engineers, attorneys), organizations that represent the interests of particular businesses (e.g., automobile dealers or clothing manufacturers), and organizations formed around recreational or intellectual interests (e.g., running, mountain climbing, chess, a particular author's work). These organizations serve important functions, but they may not be oriented toward the public interest or public service values. The mission of many other nonprofit organizations, however, is to provide services to the public that are of general benefit and have the potential to improve society. People who work in these organizations often have a passionate commitment to public service and making a difference in the world.

There are significant differences between the roles of professionals in the nonprofit and public sectors that affect how they respond to changing conditions in the political and economic environment. One of these is the relationship between professional staff and governing bodies. In earlier chapters, this relationship in the public sector has been discussed using concepts such as neutrality, politics and administration, lawfulness, and accountability. These concepts take on different meanings in the nonprofit sector, because the members of a board of directors, unlike the members of public-sector governing bodies, are not elected, they do not represent all the people in a defined area, and they are not subject to the same constitutional and legal requirements found in the public sector. Instead, they are chosen by other board members or staff, they reflect the mission-based or fund-raising needs of the organization, and, though they are expected to act lawfully, their actions are not subject to the same standards of transparency as those of elected leaders.

Staff people in a nonprofit organization are accountable to the members of the board of directors, but often they can act with greater independence in relation to the board than can public professionals in relation to an elected governing body. Nonprofit boards differ in degree of involvement in setting the mission and developing policy to an extent not found in the public sector. In describing the elements of effective performance by the boards of directors of nonprofit organizations, Nancy Axelrod (2005, 133) writes:

> For some, board effectiveness will look like keeping the board out of operations or the absence of dissent in the boardroom. For others, it will look like narrowing the locus of the board's work to carrying out its fiduciary obligations and reacting to management's recommendations. Others will find superior performance only when board members are meaningfully engaged in shaping institutional character, direction, and strategy.

Though in some circumstances an elected council, board, or legislature might be described as successful if it is removed from operations, avoids dissent, or waits to react to recommendations from management, this is not what the public expects from its elected leaders. They are expected to exercise oversight of operations, actively debate issues before them, and generate policy proposals or critically examine proposals from professional staff. Many boards in nonprofit organizations do all these things; the point here is that the role of the nonprofit board includes a range of options that is not characteristic of the public sector.

In a study of leadership during critical events in nonprofit organizations, Herman and Heimovics found that chief executives, board presidents, and staff all regard the chief executive as the central figure in leading the organization: "In short, all (including chief executives themselves) see the executive as centrally responsible for what happens in nonprofit organizations" (2005, 156). The authors drew the following conclusion from this research:

> We believe that two implications are indicated. One, since chief executives are going to be held responsible, they should take full control, running things as they think best. The board then becomes either the proverbial rubber stamp or a combination rubber stamp and cash cow. Obviously, there are many instances of this manipulative pattern. Alternatively, since chief executives are going to be held responsible and since they accept responsibility for mission accomplishment and public stewardship, they should work to see that boards fulfill their legal, organizational, and public roles. We believe that this second implication is the much wiser choice. (Herman and Heimovics 2005, 156)

In public sector organizations, staff are not as likely to discuss how they "work to see that" the governing body fulfills its obligations. The expectation in a democratic society is that the elected governing body holds the power to create laws and policies and the duty to supervise the work of people who carry out their decisions. We know that in practice public professionals are often deeply involved in formulating the laws and policies enacted by elected officials and that elected officials depend on professional expertise to understand the complex issues they deal with. Nevertheless, in the end, the constitutional/legal context and public expectations put elected governing bodies in the superior position, responsible for ensuring that public agencies and professionals are fulfilling their obligations.

Effects of a Specific Organizational Setting

Challenging conditions in the political and economic environment of public service can have very different effects on public professionals across organizations or communities. The federal and state governments are large and complex, so it is difficult to generalize about the working environment of individual professionals beyond the overall effects of conditions that impact the entire sector. The same can be said of working environments in the nonprofit sector and in local government; there is a wide range of working environments, so that from one person to the next, the daily experience of professional work can be very different indeed.

The fact that individual experiences with the working environment can be very different is not to say the differences are unimportant or that we cannot find useful ways to examine them. Three aspects of the public service environment are discussed below that can help in applying public service values to current issues in the workplace. (This material is adapted from Box 1998, 62–65.)

The first aspect is *an accessible and open or excluding and closed governance system.* This is a measure of the extent to which citizens can find information about policy making and administration and participate directly in decisions that affect them. Even in very large systems like federal agencies, there are avenues for participation such as offering commentary during rule-making processes and participating in advocacy groups. At the community level, access is much easier, though it varies from place to place. Some communities establish welcoming citizen involvement programs, while in others public input is largely limited to attending public hearings or contacting an elected official. These differences may reflect the extent to which power and influence are centralized in a community and how much residents and people working in government care about the value of participativeness.

A second aspect of the environmental context is *the prevailing attitude about the role of government in society*. We are familiar with debates about this at the national level, going back to the Founding Era, but states and communities differ along this dimension as well. Some states are known for collective decision making and a progressive approach to governance, while others are known for preferring little government involvement in public issues. The same is true at the local level. Some communities have an active, involved citizenry that uses its governmental organizations as vehicles for addressing issues and building a sense of community. In such places, local government may be involved in programs dealing with, for example, green energy, environmentally sensitive transportation alternatives, homelessness, and neighborhood participation in setting annual budget priorities. In other communities, people prefer a small, relatively passive government that only provides basic services, while the nonprofit sector works on some of the issues that government does not address.

Acceptance of, or resistance to, public professionalism is a third aspect of the environmental context of public service organizations. In some public service organizations, the political environment supports professional expertise, rational decision making, and full and open discussion of issues and alternatives. In others, professionals are expected to remain largely quiet and hidden from view, available to carry out policy directives and to make decisions based on predetermined policies and criteria. The contrast between the working environments of organizations at polar ends of a continuum of acceptance of or resistance to professionalism can be dramatic. At one end, professionals are engaged with citizens and elected leaders in examining better ways to serve public needs and to improve existing policies and procedures. At the other end professionals in understaffed agencies are hesitant to speak to anyone about public programs and issues because of the political consequences.

In any of these environmental settings, orientation toward the three aspects (governance system, role of government, role of professionals) can change over time because of elections, changes in the demographic characteristics of the population, the influence of external events locally, nationally, or globally, or other factors. The potential for these three aspects to affect the working environment of public professionals is clearly significant. However, not everyone in the same organization will respond the same way, because each person makes individual choices about which public service values are most important.

PROFESSIONAL INTEGRITY AND THE CASE OF PARK WOODS

If no workplace situations presented challenges to the values of public professionals, integrity would not be a concern. However, organizational hierarchies can make demands that conflict with these values. For example, a supervisor may ask that forms or records show the agency in a more positive light than seems appropriate; elected leaders may adopt policies that benefit their political allies while harming ordinary people; decisions about compensation and promotion may be made that seem unfair or inequitable; or operational policies or procedures may conflict with good professional practices.

Conflicts such as these can test a professional's integrity, prompting her or him to go beyond feeling an internal sense of disapproval or concern by expressing that concern to others and asking that changes be made. Challenging the status quo can be risky, with potential consequences ranging from minor to significant. As we found in the Chapter 5 section on public interest as a source of accountability, the sense of conflict between integrity and organizational demands can be so serious that a professional might choose to violate policy or become a whistleblower. This is unusual, though; in most situations the choice to be made is whether to discuss the troublesome situation with others, acting within the organizational hierarchy to resolve the issue.

Barbara Killinger (2010, 12) describes integrity as "a personal choice, an uncompromising and predictably consistent commitment to honour moral, ethical, spiritual, and artistic values and principles." This is a demanding standard, requiring strength and vigilance. Killinger wants public professionals to stretch beyond their current, comfortable outlook: "To possess integrity, we must be willing to resist the temptation to focus selectively only on information or aspects that fit our own experience, self-serving needs, or narrowly held views" (2010, 12). This is a demanding standard of behavior as well, moving the idea of integrity beyond consistency with current personal values and self-interest. It suggests that public professionals should examine the values they use to decide whether to challenge conditions around them, making changes in those values as needed.

Park Woods

We can use a brief case study to illustrate the potential for conflict between professional values such as integrity and organizational imperatives. In some ways, this case is similar to the case of the City of Micro discussed in Chapter 5. This case, though, directly addresses an organizational challenge to integrity.

Jill Gardner is the planning director for the small city of Park Woods. She is asked to assume additional responsibility, managing the unit that performs building inspections in addition to directing the planning department. There had been staff turnover in the building department because the unit had made some unreasonable demands of local business owners who wanted to remodel their properties, asking them to make improvements that were not required by local regulations. Jill is now tasked by the city administrator and city council with integrating the planning and building functions and making the building unit more resident-friendly. A new chief building inspector is hired and Jill and the inspector are asked to report back to the council in six months on progress made, with a recommendation on whether to continue the combination. The council will then decide what to do on a permanent basis.

Things go well during the interim period. The new inspector works cooperatively with the public, the planning department and building inspection unit create a new single-stop application form and process, and staff people in the two units work well together. Before the interim combination, the building inspection function was part of the public works department. There, it was one among several functioning units, it was not directly related to the engineering, construction, and maintenance orientation of public works, and it connected only indirectly with the planning department. The new combination seems to work smoothly, making things easier for citizens and creating a more immediate and logical hierarchical relationship.

So far, so good, we might think. However, there is organizational trouble on the horizon. The Park Woods city council is divided between two groups. One consists of longtime residents who are wary of public professionals, change, and new, progressive ideas. The other group on the council is, in contrast, interested in new and progressive ideas. These people want to involve citizens in setting the city's course, and they appreciate professional knowledge and expertise.

In Park Woods, the mayor has the power to hire and fire the city administrator and department heads, with approval of the city council. The mayor, part of the old guard, disapproves of city planning, the planning director, and the new combination of the planning department and building inspection unit. One day, a week or so before the city council meeting at which Jill Gardner and the chief inspector are to give their six-month report on the new combination, the city administrator calls Jill to his office. The administrator explains that the mayor has given an order that the report will say the combination is of little value and it would be just as well to return the building unit to its old home in public works. The mayor has made it clear that the city administrator's job depends on this result, and if Jill does not do as she is told, her time in Park Woods will be short as well.

Jill is surprised at what she considers to be a direct order to lie about organizational operations. Whether or not the planning/building combination is a good idea could be a matter of perspective, but the mayor wants the facts to be distorted, suppressing information about successful achievement of goals and downplaying advantages. Jill expresses her discomfort about what appears to be an unethical and improper order, but the administrator restates that both his job and Jill's are at stake. A few days later, Jill shares this dilemma with two council members from the progressive wing of the council. They urge her to report truthfully, but they do not think they can shield her from retribution by the mayor.

So Park Woods is now the scene of a value-laden challenge to professional integrity. It is easy enough from a distance to say what should be done, but in this case there are two important sets of public service values in opposition. The elected chief executive of the city, the mayor, has given a clear and direct order to his subordinates, one that he presumably thinks is in the public interest. The planner, Jill Gardner, is worried that complying with the order would seriously damage her sense of integrity, because her public actions would be in conflict with her professional values.

On one side, we find honesty, professionalism, and integrity, and on the other, loyalty, neutrality, obedience, and organizational interest. Accountability can be found on either side of the issue, with accountability to the profession on one side and accountability to duly constituted authority on the other.

If you were in Jill's position, what would you do? There seem to be three options: comply with the mayor's order, suppressing the facts and leaving the council to make a decision based on a false impression of what has actually occurred; give an honest assessment, with a recommendation to continue the combination; or give an honest report about what has been done but omit the recommendation, leaving the council to draw its own conclusion about whether continuing the combination is desirable. The first option is a threat to Jill Gardner's integrity, the second option carries serious career risks for Jill and for the city administrator, and the third seems incomplete, if safer. How can the competing values be reconciled in a way that preserves Jill's sense of integrity? Are there values that are more important than integrity in this situation?

Individual Judgment

However we might answer these questions, the Park Woods case highlights the potential for conflict between professional and organizational values. Such a conflict can challenge public professionals to closely examine which public service values are most important to them. Terry Cooper (2012, 35–37) describes a decision-making process for ethical dilemmas such as this one. The process includes a "rehearsal of defenses," in which a person considers the consequences of alternative courses of action, including what it would be like to publicly defend a particular decision or to have it reported in the media. This process involves creating a "movie in our minds" (37), in which we imagine whether or not we would be satisfied with the likely outcomes of alternative choices. Ultimately, "resolution is reached when we discover an alternative that provides an acceptable balance of our duty to principle and the likely consequences and satisfies our need to have sound reasons for our conduct and our need to feel satisfied with the decision" (36). Using such a process, we can imagine the effects on public service values and our sense of integrity in a difficult situation like the one in Park Woods and also in other less serious but nevertheless challenging circumstances.

The relationship between professional integrity and the demands of the organization and its environment varies from person to person. The occupational example of Park Woods and its city planner can be used to show that judgments about professional integrity are specific to the person and situation. We can imagine another hypothetical city, in which development is rapid and poorly regulated, so that the impacts may be passed on to present and future residents in the form of pollution, traffic congestion, poor water quality, and crumbling infrastructure. In this setting, a planner whose professional judgment is that economic growth and development are primary goals and that environmental sustainability is secondary might think things are going well. Business thrives, jobs are being created, and people are optimistic about the future. In that same city, a planner in whose professional judgment a sustainable environment and economy are primary might think significant damage is being done and that action needs to be taken to reduce the influence of the development community on the governing process.

The first planner, for whom economic growth and development are primary, may not experience significant challenges to professional integrity, because the planner's values are compatible with those of the organization. For the second planner, the potential for challenges to integrity is substantial, because the organization

and the political environment may require the planner to emphasize development over sustainability in a way that violates deeply
held beliefs about planning and development. Using a technique
such as Cooper's "movie in our mind" may help identify points of
agreement or conflict between professional values and organizational demands. This may allow time to reflect on which values
are most important and how to achieve a satisfactory resolution
of value conflicts while preserving integrity.

MAKING A DIFFERENCE: THE PUBLIC PROFESSIONAL AS AGENT OF CHANGE

In *The Moral Imagination and Public Life: Raising the Ethical Question*, Thomas McCollough (1991) asks a fascinating question that at
first glance seems odd: "What is my personal relation to what I know?"
McCollough wants us to consider whether we have a responsibility
to take action because we are aware of conditions in society that are
not good for people, the world, or the public interest. Public professionals who go beyond thinking about this question to take action
are no longer guided by the value of neutrality; other values have
proved to be more important, at least in a particular situation.

The introduction to this chapter noted that some public professionals feel a commitment or inspiration to make the world a better
place. Such a commitment is unique to each person, depending on
occupation, organization, and personal background. The common
element is that those who experience it are thinking about conditions outside themselves, something larger than the individual and
self-interest. Making a difference is transformational, meaning that
it changes some part of the world in a real and noticeable way,
so it is not the same as it was before. According to Cheryl Simrell
King and Lisa Zanetti (drawing from the work of O.C. McSwite),
the commitment to making a difference comes from a "personally
grounded social concern" (2005, 91). Transformation begins with
this concern and it can be large or small; King and Zanetti write,
"We are not necessarily talking about great leadership or doing
great things, but about doing the daily, basic things mindfully and
with commitment, compassion, and passion" (91).

Thinking that one might act on what one knows, with a commitment to transformation and making a difference, sounds a bit vague and flowery. What does it mean in the daily context of professional public service? Each of the six actions below describes a specific, useful technique for putting a commitment to making a difference into practice. (The first five items are adapted from Box 2007b, 202–208, and the last from Box 2011, 71–73.) In its own way, each item shows public professionals acting as agents of change, a role that moves away from neutrality and can, in some circumstances, test the boundaries of accountability.

Sense and Describe Needs

This category of action is basic to the professional role. It involves gathering and analyzing information about current conditions immediately related to organizational mission, in addition to broader knowledge of best practices, alternative futures, and trends in social and environmental change. Though the collection and display of information may seem value-neutral, apolitical, and uncontroversial, the sorts of knowledge gathered may call into question ways an organization operates in relation to issues such as efficiency, social equity, rational versus political decision making, and use of governmental authority by powerful groups and individuals.

In addition, the process of gathering information may include interacting with individual citizens and groups, potentially bringing the practitioner in conflict with elected officials or political appointees who worry that the practitioner may be developing an independent constituency. Citizens, elected officials, or the practitioner may find it difficult to distinguish professional from political activity in interaction with citizens; is this a matter of gathering information or of helping people recognize and define needs and preferences?

Modify Operating Procedures

Within the organization, practitioners may modify operating procedures in ways that serve specific values. Of course, public service practitioners function within a legal and institutional order that constrains their actions, and they have a duty to the public to remain faithful to these constraints. However, it would be very difficult to screen out public service values, becoming a value-free automaton carrying out orders.

Though it is possible to suppress creativity, imagination, and empathy in public employees by assigning mind-numbing work or threatening negative consequences for deviation from the official line, every professional sees the world through a particular set of personal and professional values. Within the constraints of the legal and institutional order, there is considerable room for independent judgment and action. The daily work of a police chief or state human services manager, for example, proceeds within the role expectations of the given position.

Within their role expectations, these people apply personal and professional experience, values, and standards of performance as they intentionally or unintentionally shape both policy and the environment in which it is created and changed over time. They establish and modify operating procedures, shift staff and material resources among areas, and communicate their values and concerns to agency staff. In these ways, public service values become part of their daily work.

Propose Programs and Policies

This category of practitioner action follows the "sense and describe needs" category above, using gathered information to bridge the gap between professional knowledge and the relevant governing body or bodies. It is part of the action loop that includes aggregation of interests that rise to the level of the public policy agenda; a period of public discourse; a decision that adopts a policy; implementation; and feedback on progress, potentially leading to policy modification.

The public professional formulates a recommendation for change to be presented, possibly with intermediate steps in the hierarchy, to the ultimate decision maker. This could be a cabinet secretary at the national or state levels, Congress or a state legislature, the board of a nonprofit organization, or city or county

administrators or governing bodies. Making any policy recommendation can carry risk of resistance from defenders of the status
quo. The professional making a recommendation will consider the
risk and potential benefits, deciding whether the public service
values being served outweigh potential consequences.

Provide Information to the Public

This action category focuses on spanning the boundary of the
organization and linking with citizens. As noted above, acquisition of knowledge can present risks, and making it available to
the public at large magnifies that potential. However, providing
citizens with as much information as possible about current conditions, best practices, and alternative futures is closely linked to
values such as transparency, participativeness, and democracy.
To the extent that citizens choose to become informed about and
involved in the policy process, they need a full range of information and interpretation.

Provide Meaningful Access to Policy Processes

It is difficult for many people to take part in the traditional public
policy process for a variety of reasons, including lack of knowledge about government, the cost of time needed to acquire information and participate, and lifestyle, work commitments, and
personal interests. The national government was not created to
promote participation by individual citizens, and individual participation at the state level is not much easier. Those who participate
often do so through membership in large advocacy organizations.
At the local level there can be greater potential for involvement,
though access may be limited by organizational size, complexity
of processes, or political or administrative attitudes about citizen
influence in decision making.

Despite the potential barriers to citizen involvement in policy
making, there are times and places in which public professionals and elected officials welcome and encourage it. As an
ideal, public service professionals ensure that participatory
processes and settings (electronic as well as traditional meet-

ings and face-to-face dialogue) are as understandable, open, transparent, and welcoming as possible. Providing such settings may require advocacy and persuasion within the organization and may entail some risk of opposition and failure. However, the potential benefits in relation to public service values are considerable.

Imagine Alternative Futures

Imagining alternative futures is a way to shape future conditions rather than waiting for them to happen. This is not an unusual or exotic technique, and it is used with tools such as strategic planning, scenario planning, and land-use planning. To use an example found in many communities, planners and local residents may be concerned about the rate, form, cost, and environmental impacts of physical growth in housing and commercial land use. A number of techniques may be used to manage growth and minimize negative impacts, but in any one community residents and elected leaders may not be aware of them. This means it is left to public professionals to assemble data on local growth, gather information on growth management practices in other places, and show several alternative futures for the community that depend on a range of different policy options.

An alternative futures analysis might show a scenario with growth spread throughout a large area, another with several distributed population nodes, and another that concentrates dense development along light rail transportation corridors. For each alternative future, the analysis would provide projections for traffic flows, costs of providing infrastructure, air pollution, social conditions in the central city, and so on.

This example sets the technique of imagining alternative futures in the context of community planning, but it can be applied effectively in nonprofit organizations and at all levels of government, in settings with citizen involvement and in settings where only professionals, or professionals and elected leaders, assess current conditions and plan for future actions. Examining practices from other places or organizations, along with open discussion of alternative futures, helps avoid status quo thinking that replicates present circumstances instead of consciously choosing a desired future.

VALUES ASSOCIATED WITH PUBLIC SERVICE

As discussed throughout this book, many values can be linked to the core value of public service. Some interrelated values deserve additional attention here. They connect with McCollough's question, "What is my personal relation to what I know?" and they prompt us to consider how our thoughts and actions affect those we serve. Six of these values are *benevolence, compassion, dignity, fairness, humaneness,* and *tolerance.* Taken together, they reflect an attitude of identification with and acceptance of others, including those who are in some ways different from us. They also express a desire to serve others in a helpful way, to respect their dignity, and to avoid bias and injustice.

It would be easy enough to reject these values as mushy and sentimental and to wall them off in our minds from the practical daily work of delivering public services. The world can be a tough and demanding place. For those who must deal with political or public irrationality, physical threat, economic pressures, or difficult clientele and problems, these values may seem remote and unrelated to the work that needs to be done. (Think of the roles of police officers and judges, people who manage complicated contracts with private companies, military officers, social service workers with huge caseloads, and so on.)

However, it is exactly because of conditions in the world and professional commitments to public service and making a difference that these values matter. A public service that carries out the law mechanically and without regard for its effects on people and the physical environment may serve the value of neutrality well, but fail to address other values that are important to society. Benevolence, compassion, dignity, fairness, humaneness, and tolerance can be organized around the core value of *empathy,* which Lisa Zanetti (2011, 78) describes as "the ability to identify with another individual." Zanetti's case for empathy as central to public service is compelling:

Public service is a public trust. If we see public administrators as trustees of the public interest or ethical citizen-administrators charged with using moral imagination, then undoubtedly empathy is a foundational value. . . . We seldom see outright calls for empathy as a working value—yet arguably it is empathy that provides the foundation for altruism, tolerance, benevolence, and, by extension, public service. (84)

APPLYING THE VALUE OF PUBLIC SERVICE IN PROFESSIONAL LIFE

The narrative of this chapter includes an examination of characteristics of human behavior and the societal environment surrounding professional public service, and it discusses preserving one's sense of professional integrity while dealing with challenging, complex issues. How each of us uses knowledge of societal conditions around us is a matter of individual judgment, unique to each person, organization, and specific situation. This is a matter of sorting through relevant values and deciding what is most important to us at a particular point in time.

A brief case example can be used to illustrate values in action. This case tells the story of a branch manager in a state social welfare system who brings about significant change in the way her organization serves the public. She does this entirely within existing laws and policies and the role she is expected to fill in the state bureaucracy. However, this person has a clear commitment to making a difference, and her choices are value-driven.

As you read the case, consider how values such as neutrality, efficiency, accountability, personal commitment to public service, making a difference, empathy, and others we have discussed are in evidence in the program changes made by the branch manager. The case study recounts events in a way that makes it seem the changes were made in a smooth, linear manner, but that is not how such things usually happen. There were probably times when staff people resisted the changes or when some community residents thought the branch manager's actions favored people who were undeserving. How do you think the branch manager might have handled such challenges, while retaining a sense of integrity between deeply held values and the possibilities for action in the community?

The Branch Manager

Imagine a newly appointed branch manager within a state social welfare system. The branch is in a part of the state far away from major population centers and has been run for decades in a quite traditional way, with the staff divided into functional assistance areas such as housing, food, medical care, work training, and disability. There have been attempts at centralizing intake processes across functional areas, but they have had limited success in streamlining the overall experience for clients. Staff members are oriented toward the requirements in law and policy of their particular areas of specialization and that is what they do best. The result is that clients often spend many hours, even days, working their way through the various parts of the system that apply to them. To the extent efficiencies exist in cross-communication, they tend to be specific to a particular client's situation and the result of a staff person's effort to "do a favor" for a client.

The new branch manager dislikes treating clients as if their time has no value, putting them through lots of red tape just because that is how it has always been done. On a broader level, she wants to change how people in this rural community think about and deal with the issue of social inequality. Working with staff, she designs and implements a new organizational structure focused on the client as a whole person rather than on the bureaucracy. Now, a person who comes to the agency for services is greeted by a staff member who is trained to assess how the organization might improve the client's life and chances for working upward out of the social welfare system. That staff person remains the client's primary contact, taking responsibility for coordinating with staff in functional areas to deliver services. The time spent by clients interacting with the agency has been cut dramatically, the fit between clients and services has improved, and overall staff time spent in client interaction has decreased significantly.

In addition to these internal improvements, the new branch manager reaches out to the community to make the agency's new approach visible to potential clients and community leaders. This is accomplished by having staff distribute flyers in shelters, restaurants, and churches, and the manager speaks to meetings of community business, civic, and religious groups. As a result, the agency is serving more clients, and poverty, homelessness, and inequality have become part of the civic dialogue in a way they were not before, resulting in some new initiatives in the nonprofit sector to address these problems.

Lessons Learned

The branch manager's ideas are not new. They have been used in other places, but in this remote area they are somewhat startling. Residents are not accustomed to speaking openly about social services and the effects of inequality, nor do they expect a state bureaucrat to lead in creating a community dialogue on these issues. By bringing to her new position professional concepts unfamiliar in this setting and acting within the existing framework of policy and practice, the branch manager is able to create meaningful change that advances her values. She has sensed needs, imagined an alternative future, modified operating procedures, and provided information to the public. We could add the value of participativeness to the case study by having the branch manager create a citizen's advisory group to assist with the change process.

Aside from keeping her superior in the state capital aware of the changes being made in branch operations, the manager does not need to seek policy changes or approval of her plans. Instead, she works comfortably within the space between doing what has always been done and violating existing policy or accepted practice. Put another way, she advances public service values and serves as an agent of change while remaining within the role boundaries expected for her position. (This case first appeared in Box 2008, 91–92; it is presented here with modifications to fit the theme of this chapter.)

7

The Public Interest

Commitment to Society

THE MEANING OF PUBLIC INTEREST

The idea of public interest appears in many places in public affairs. It can be found in legislation directing a commission, board, or agency head to act in the public interest, in statements people make about why they want to take a particular action ("it is in the public interest!"), and in scholarly research. The idea sounds so reasonable and constructive that often we do not think to examine what it means, but finding a specific meaning can be difficult.

Walter Lippmann, commenting on the public interest in 1922, said it was what people would do "if they saw clearly, thought rationally, acted disinterestedly and benevolently" (quoted in Cooper 2012, 81). This does not take us much closer to the public interest, since often people do not have enough information to clearly understand the circumstances they face, decision-making processes are often a matter of emotion and compromise rather than rationality, and almost by definition politics and complex public decisions involve individual and group interests, along with difficulty in treating others benevolently, with kindness and goodwill.

Several years after Lippmann commented on the idea of public interest, in 1936 E. Pendleton Herring wrote, "The *public interest* is the standard that guides the administrator in executing the law. This is the verbal symbol designed to introduce unity, order, and objectivity into administration" (1997, 78). This seems promising;

few would argue against a verbal symbol that may yield unity, order, and objectivity. However, Herring followed this thought by observing, "To hold out the public interest as a criterion is to offer an imponderable. Its value is psychological and does not extend beyond the significance that each responsible civil servant must find in the phrase for himself" (78). So we are back where we began, with the public interest as an elusive concept that takes on different meanings from person to person.

Beginning in the 1950s, the concept of public interest experienced a withering critique from scholars of public affairs. Glendon Schubert was a prominent voice in this critique; he found that writers in public administration were unable to construct a usable description of "how the public interest is defined in administrative decision-making," and they had failed to develop theories to explain "the actual behavior of real people" (1957, 366). He concluded that the idea of public interest is mostly a "datum of politics" (1960, 223), a thought that would occasionally appear in discussion of public issues but that has no specific meaning.

Not everyone shared this view. During the same time period, Gerhard Colm (1962, 127) rose to the defense of the public interest: "The vague concept of the public interest loses much of its vagueness as a result of political debates, judicial interpretations, and translations into specific goals of economic performance and achievement. As a matter of fact, it is difficult to imagine that politicians, statesmen, judges, and officials concerned with the formulation of government policies could do without this concept."

Since this debate about the public interest several decades ago, authors have been careful to acknowledge that the concept is difficult to define. Nevertheless, it continues to be important, not just in academic writing, but in the work of decision makers, administrators, and citizens participating in public affairs. Deborah Stone (2002, 21) offers four possible meanings of public interest. The first is "individual interests held in common, things everyone wants for themselves, such as a high standard of living." The second meaning is "individual goals for the community." These goals can conflict with what people want for themselves: "They want good schools and clean air, perhaps, but also lower taxes and the right to burn their trash." A third meaning of public interest is "those goals on which there is a consensus," such as "programs and policies favored by a majority of citizens." An important feature of this meaning of public interest is that "the public interest is not necessarily enduring. It is whatever most people want at the moment, and so it changes over time." Stone's final meaning is "things that are good for a community as a community." This includes "its own sense of order and fair play," "some governing processes," "some means of resolving disputes without violence," and "an interest in [community] survival," which means "defense against outsiders" (Stone 2002, 21).

Stone's third meaning—programs and policies favored by a majority—is especially useful in policy making and implementation. The idea of public interest reflects one side of the tension between private interest and public purpose discussed in Chapter 4. It focuses on collective goals and actions, giving people involved in public affairs an opportunity to imagine what the future could be like.

Barry Bozeman contrasts the idea of public interest with market interest, arguing that, because the private economy does not deal with "all values important to a society. . . . almost all concede the need for both a government role and public values that are not fully contained in market values" (2007, 97). Bozeman identifies five categories of public interest: formal, substantive, aggregational, procedural, and normative (96). For our purposes we can use three perspectives on public interest. First, in an *aggregate* perspective, the public interest is the sum of the existing views of the most powerful groups or the majority of individuals. Group interests can be expressed through political debates, and individual views can be measured with surveys or through voting. Second, a *process* perspective focuses on how people find the public interest together. This is about who participates, what sort of discussion occurs, and how responsibility for making decisions is allocated. The third perspective is *substantive*, with the goal of identifying what people mean in a particular situation when they refer to the public interest.

The aggregate perspective on the public interest is central to political decision making, but the process and substantive perspectives are especially important in public service. Many public professionals become involved in helping identify service needs and program and policy changes—this is about the process of finding the public interest rather than describing its meaning. Carol Lewis (2006, 696) writes, "As a public service duty, the public interest is conceptualized more fruitfully as a process, not as an objectively identifiable endpoint. An elusive and sweeping obligation, it is a never-ending process that is made meaningful more by practice than by a product." Denhardt and Denhardt (2011, 73) echo this view: "It is, as the saying goes, more a journey than a destination." A number of public service values seem related to the process perspective, such as neutrality, accountability, professionalism, rule of law, transparency, and integrity.

The substantive perspective is also a key part of public service. When public professionals act on particular values, they are expressing a view of the public interest. Examples of values that appear to be expressions of substantive public interest are democracy, sustainability, tolerance, and social justice. Some other values seem related to both the process and substantive perspectives, such as benevolence, inclusiveness, representativeness, participativeness, efficiency, and effectiveness.

A working definition of public interest tailored to the discussion of public service values will help in organizing our thoughts. The definition is: "The future that a majority of people would choose at a particular point in time, given adequate information and an opportunity for dialogue with others before making a decision." In the three sections directly below, this definition is separated into parts, connecting it with three public service values: *participativeness*, *representativeness*, and *transparency*. These sections are process-oriented; they are followed in the section on values associated with the public interest by discussion of a substantive value important in professional practice, social equity.

PARTICIPATIVENESS: THE PUBLIC INTEREST OVER TIME

Participativeness is about the extent of commitment by public professionals to the idea that citizens should have opportunities to participate in decision making about public policies and programs. There are many ways citizens can be directly involved in creating policies and programs, such as serving on a task force, citizen's committee, neighborhood group, and so on. The Chapter 2 section on democracy as a source of values discusses citizen involvement as a way to enhance democratic governance.

People can engage with government as customers receiving services, as partners in service delivery (e.g., separating recyclables), or directly, as citizens sharing responsibility for decision making. Which role is appropriate is a matter of the type of service or government action and whether direct citizen involvement would further the ends of a public agency and benefit the larger community (Thomas 2012). John Clayton Thomas writes that public professionals may fear direct public involvement because it could be costly and inefficient. As a result, "many public managers have sought to avoid public involvement. They would be better advised to view public involvement as a contingent proposition. Public involvement in making decisions will be desirable under some circumstances, but not others, and the extent of involvement desirable will also vary with the circumstances" (2012, 7).

In addition, some people worry that direct citizen involvement in decision making could threaten the public interest, if citizen demands overwhelm government or interest groups "capture" the "agendas and programs of specific agencies to the neglect of the broader public interest" (Thomas 2012, 211). As we might expect, there are situations in which these negative effects are apparent, but citizen involvement has not proven to be a threat to "the well-being of society as a whole" (210).

A commitment to democracy and participativeness suggests that decision makers should be ready to involve the public whenever this is useful in supporting a decision-making process. Such a commitment can lead to a welcoming attitude toward citizen input and a stronger and more productive relationship between the public and government. Camilla Stivers (1990, 265) describes the importance of this relationship as a matter of public interest and accountability:

> A substantive public decision-making role for citizens is important as a mechanism for constructing a shared understanding of the public interest. . . . Justification of agency actions . . . becomes tied to a

practice of accountability, as administrators fulfill the obligation to give good reasons and take citizens' expressed views seriously.

A key part of participativeness and decision making about the public interest is the element of time; as Deborah Stone (2002, 21) notes, because the public interest is whatever most people want at the moment, it can change with the passage of time. Today's majority view of the public interest need not forever deny people who disagree with it the possibility of making their conception of the public interest the one that guides decision making later on.

It may be comforting to believe there is a single public interest to be found, but a crisp, clear view of the public interest is rare. In its absence, people find acceptable substitutes by discussing current circumstances, action options, and possible outcomes. They decide what to do and later on may revisit a decision as they discover how it works in practice. If we think about today's view of public interest in a given situation (such as deciding on national security policy, which new highway to build, or how much money to spend on a new school), it is "cross-sectional, one point in a timeline of different, consecutive views of the public interest that appear in the public policy process and the laws, policies, and operating practices that result" (Box 2008, 61). Though it is the dominant view today, the current description of the public interest may be ill-suited to conditions in the future, since

> it is known to be imperfect, alternatives are and will become available, and circumstances in the political, economic, or physical environment will change. When the current image outlives its usefulness, causing inefficiency, damage, public resistance, excessive cost, etc., a new dialogue will emerge and a new image will be adopted. (Box 2007a, 596)

This potential for change in the public interest over time is a good thing for social stability, a healthy democracy, and efficient administration, because

> a public interest that changes slowly or not at all disregards the interests of those who disagree with it, so it is a recipe for discontent and conflict. With a relatively static, fixed public interest, laws or operating practices would be adopted based on a description of the public interest

that may soon be superseded by changes in societal conditions, but the "old" description would remain in place. This gives people who may be the losers in a policy debate an incentive to resist compromise or agreement, for fear the result will be long lasting. (Box 2008, 61)

Another important thing about participativeness is the potential for personal growth and transformation, since each person's perspective can change in the process of dialogue with others. Political or market models of citizens may characterize them as holding fixed views that can influence public policy, for example when people respond to opinion polls or when they vote. In contrast, when people take part in dialogue with other citizens and with professional staff or elected leaders, their views may change. As I put it several years ago,

> the process view of the public interest regards individuals as participants in dialogue about what is in the public interest and what the public sector should do about it. Instead of packages of pre-determined interests, individuals are perceived as people with interests who can learn from social interaction. In such interactions, they acquire new information about public issues and become aware of the perceptions and desires of others. They may find their interests changing or, even if their interests do not change, they may be willing to compromise for the good of the larger community. (Box 2007a, 588–589)

In sum, participativeness means that citizens are directly involved in decision-making processes and that individual views of the public interest can change during interaction with others. A particular conception of the public interest also contains the possibility of change, because the conditions that support it can be different in the future from what they are today. This is a good thing, because it allows democratic dialogue on the public interest to continue, reshaping the public interest and the tools used to implement it so they fit current needs and circumstances.

REPRESENTATIVENESS: IMAGINING THE PUBLIC INTEREST

Any of several reasons could explain why the public is not directly involved in decision making by elected leaders or professional staff in a particular situation. Many governmental decision-making processes are not well suited to citizen involvement because they are about technical or routine matters that would not interest most members of the public. In other situations where the public might have an interest in shaping programs or policies, there may be barriers to direct citizen involvement.

Here are examples of barriers to citizen involvement: a public agency's complex systems may be relatively inaccessible to individual citizens or citizen groups; its staff may not make it easy for people to participate; there may be no organized paths for participation; citizens may not care enough about policy outcomes to volunteer to participate; there may be a public perception that the policy process is controlled by business or political leaders, so what the people as a whole want does not count; people may be too busy to volunteer; people may be aware they can give money to interest groups but they know little or nothing about direct participation.

Whatever the reasons, often a current view of the public interest is identified not by citizens but by elected leaders and/or public professionals. It is not unusual for elected leaders and their career staff to make significant decisions without organized, direct input from citizens:

> It has become a cliché in American society that members of the public are indifferent, or even hostile, to government and politics. Voting rates are low, anti-government attitudes are frequently expressed in the media (talk radio is an extreme example), bureaucrat bashing is commonplace, and the public service is regarded by many with disdain. Elected officials, public professionals, and citizens who are aware of or involved in matters of governance often consider the public to be largely incapable of forming intelligent judgments about public affairs. If public involvement in governing is, or should be, restricted to the periodic act of voting because of apathy or incapacity, then governing is solely the province of elected leaders, their appointees, and public professionals. (Box 2005, 127)

Important choices made about programs or policies can clearly affect the public interest, but routine workplace actions may do so as well, such as improving record keeping in aircraft inspections, finding cost-efficient methods to extend the life of new roadways, or reducing administrative expenses for mental-health counseling services. Whenever we take action, we are intentionally choosing a particular outcome. Whether the result is exactly what we intended is a separate issue, but we have in mind a particular goal that could make the future better, in ways large or small.

A key element in choosing an alternative in the public interest is *imagination*. In the classic model of public sector accountability (see the section on accountability to elected leaders and organizational superiors in Chapter 5), elected leaders decide on the public interest, based at least in part on their perception of what citizens want, and public professionals implement that vision. Sometimes decision making and action follow this path. Often, though, it is career staff rather than politicians who use their knowledge of on-the-ground conditions and interactions with the public to imagine how service delivery and its effects could be improved. They use this knowledge to take action themselves or to suggest policy changes to legislators. In the Chapter 2 section on democracy as a source of values, the concept of "imagining private lives" described the application of professional knowledge to imagine the impacts administrative action can have on conditions in society. In Chapter 6, the discussion of "imagining alternative futures" suggested one way that public professionals could serve as agents of change.

When public professionals imagine what the future could be, they are representing the public and shaping the public interest. Though this form of representation challenges the common understanding of professional neutrality and accountability in a democratic society, in the real world this is often how things work. This means that representativeness, as a public service value, can be relevant to public professionals as well as to elected leaders and political appointees.

TRANSPARENCY: PROVIDING FULL INFORMATION

Transparency in public service organizations can be complicated and even dramatic. We can readily think of examples in which government's desire to control information was challenged by people determined to weaken that control: the release in 1971 by Daniel Ellsberg of the "Pentagon Papers" describing actions of the United States regarding South Vietnam and other countries in the region; the Watergate political scandal of the early 1970s, involving a cover-up by the Nixon administration; and the controversy about government surveillance of personal communications provoked by the 2013 release of secret documents by Edward Snowden.

In addition to these high-profile situations in which people have pushed government to be more transparent, there are national and state laws that allow citizen access to information held by public agencies. The Freedom of Information Act, passed in 1966, allows access to federal government information, and states have laws requiring transparency of information and in the conduct of public meetings. Both of these ways of making government more transparent—dramatic releases of information and laws requiring some degree of transparency—can be important to democracy. In this discussion, though, we want to focus on the public professional's contribution to transparency in the creation and implementation of policies and programs.

The concept of a "helper" role for public professionals was described in Chapter 2. In this role, professionals give citizens the information they need to assist with informed decision making, and they facilitate dialogue between citizens and between citizens and agency staff and leaders on policy-related issues. There are risks associated with this role. Because not all elected leaders and staff approve of public professionals giving citizens access to information held by public agencies, doing so can be a cause of friction between professionals and people in their agencies. Another type of risk is that informed citizens may come to conclusions contrary to those of the public professionals who have been working with them. "For example, citizens may take a stand against construction of public housing when involved practitioners may be concerned about social equity," or a "citizen-driven policy process . . . results in development decisions that could harm the environment" (Box 1998, 145), even though public professionals want to emphasize sustainability.

A key feature of the helper role is that "helpers do not strive for greater power, autonomy, and recognition. Instead, they give away knowledge and thus the power to make decisions to the people who are affected by those decisions. Paradoxically, this giving away of control makes practitioners more rather than less effective, as community residents, informed by practitioners, understand the issues and insist on meaningful change" (Box 1998, 144–145).

As constructive as the helper role sounds, there are limits to how much can be done to provide the public with the information they need to make informed decisions. One such limit comes from the nature of knowledge, which is fragmentary and uncertain; using the Greek word for city-state, *polis*, as a substitute for "community," Deborah Stone (2002, 29) writes:

> In the polis, information is never complete. We can never know all the possible means for achieving a goal or all the possible effects of an action, especially since all actions have side effects, unanticipated consequences, and long-term effects. Nor can we know for sure what other people will do in response to our actions, yet often we choose to act on the basis of what others will do. If people act at all, they must necessarily act on guesses, hunches, expectations, hopes, and faith, as well as on facts.

In addition, according to Stone (2002, 29), "Information is never fully and equally available to all participants in politics," and "crucial information is very often deliberately kept secret" (e.g., where a city plans to locate a sewage treatment plant). Thus, "secrecy and revelation are tools of political strategy, and we would grossly misunderstand the character of information in politics if we thought of it as neutral facts, readily disclosed." Peter Bachrach and Morton Baratz (1962) argue that public knowledge of important issues, and the opportunity to act on that knowledge, can be influenced by "nondecision making," the practice of keeping issues off the public agenda to protect the advantage that knowledge gives certain leaders over other people. Taken together, resisting disclosure and keeping information from being discussed are powerful ways people can control the policy process.

Here is a brief story that illustrates the relationship of public professionals to knowledge and the public. Sometime ago, I invited some professionals from the local city to speak to my class on municipal management. One of them was the city traffic engineer. He discussed the decision he had made about timing of traffic signals on a major (eight-lane) north-south corridor street. He had decided that smooth north-south flow was of such importance that he adjusted the signal timing for east-west cross-street traffic to be as short as possible. This meant that people in cars waiting to cross the major street would wait even longer than one might ordinarily expect. (Some of these cross streets were also significant four-lane east-west arterials.)

When I questioned the engineer about the decision process on this issue, he took pride in saying that he had consulted no one else, he did not need to hear from non-experts, and he was the only person in the city qualified to make such a decision. There was no point to challenging him in class. However, in many places this would be considered a policy decision worthy of review by elected officials and citizen advisory groups. Had I been city manager of that city when I heard the engineer speak, I would probably have formed an advisory panel, including experts, citizens, and elected leaders, to review policy matters related to traffic flow. (And I would have had a talk with the engineer, later considering whether he should be transferred to another position.) From the national level (think of shuttle accidents, airport security procedures, intelligence failures, regulation of the financial sector) to the local level, oversight and informed policy making by elected bodies and citizen boards, committees, and neighborhood groups are important for democratic governance. This requires a measure of transparency, and public professionals have a role in providing it.

VALUES ASSOCIATED WITH PUBLIC INTEREST

There are many public service values associated with public interest, both in relation to process, such as transparency, and substance, such as sustainability. In addition to the values discussed in this book, there are many more connected with specific occupational specializations, such as law enforcement, environmental protection, and social services.

Not all values that matter to the idea of public interest involve taking action to change current conditions. For example, the values of neutrality, efficiency, and accountability can be used in particular situations to suggest that public professionals should implement law and policy without consciously influencing their interpretation. In these situations, the public interest involves dutiful service rather than an active role in shaping it.

Often, though, people with a commitment to public service have a view of the future that includes change they believe to be constructive for society. This may lead them to take some of the actions described in the Chapter 6 discussion of "making a difference." At this point in our discussion, it is appropriate to think about professional public service and views of the public interest that go beyond neutral obedience and duty, acknowledging the potential professional role in helping create a better future.

In earlier chapters we reviewed the historical development of the context of public service and specific aspects of the environment of professional work in the field. We found that the economic and political systems can be challenging to the work of public professionals, requiring persistence and dedication. It may not be accurate to say that contemporary times are more difficult than were earlier times—that seems to be one of those things people say in every generation—but there is no question that the list of issues to be dealt with today is long and complicated. Rodney Coates (2007, 579) offers this summary perspective:

> We live in troubled times. War and social unrest, terror and retribution, homophobia and sexual abuse, racism and xenophobia, and distrust and paranoia seem to abound. How we interpret, relate to, and indeed conceptualize these complex issues all too often seems to be determined by which side of the social divide we find ourselves. Although certainly not unique in social memory, current situations (perceptual or real) nevertheless pose unique problems for us, as we appear to go from crisis to crisis.

Because it is not possible to discuss all the current issues and values associated with public interest, we focus here on one broad, inclusive area, *social equity*, which is another way of thinking about social justice, acting in ways that result in a fairer and more just society. Three reasons can be given to support this choice: many of the more troubling issues in society are connected with injustice and inequality; interesting research on concepts and practice related to social equity has been published by public affairs scholars; and there are many things, large and small, that public professionals can do about social equity in their daily work.

The Concept of Social Equity

Social equity is broad and inclusive. It is not about a complete leveling of social class so that all people are equal in socioeconomic status. It is about shifting to some extent the distribution of resources and power in society so they are not as concentrated at the top as they are today. This involves recognition that a viable democracy requires a general citizenry that has opportunities to participate and thrive in the economic and political life of the community and the nation. A seriously unequal society, in which resources and power are held by a few to the exclusion of the many, is in danger of losing the sense of citizenship and possibility that gives people reason to support it.

Norman Johnson and James Svara (2011a, 3) describe the concept of social equity as "the promotion of equality in a society with deep social and economic disparities. It embodies the goal that the members of all social groups will have the same prospects for success and the same opportunity to be protected from the adversities of life." This sounds straightforward enough, but in reality it is a demanding standard. Johnson and Svara acknowledge that not everyone will be equal in "conditions and success," but they think differences in life circumstances between people should not be the result of one's ethnicity, race, or gender. They make a direct connection to public administration, arguing that socioeconomic status should not be related to "differences in the availability of basic public services nor to the quality of those services" (3).

Social equity is not only about economic inequality, though this is important, nor only about one particular group of people likely to suffer from discrimination or abuse. In Johnson and Svara's description, social equity addresses the possibilities all people have to improve their lives and succeed in achieving their goals, and it seeks to remove barriers that make this more difficult. We can easily get lost in the details of policy issues, such as food stamps, unemployment insurance, health care, the minimum wage, gay rights, and gender discrimination, and miss the point of social equity.

For historical and cultural reasons, there have been many examples of inequity, inequality, and injustice in the United States, such as working conditions during the Gilded Age and Progressive Era of the late nineteenth and early twentieth centuries, unemployment and living conditions of older people during the Great Depression of the 1930s, treatment of African Americans and Native Americans (Gooden 2014), and poverty and race and gender discrimination addressed by government in the 1960s and 1970s.

In contrast to the "social democracies" found in some other developed nations, the American political system is often resistant to taking thorough and effective action on these issues. In part, this resistance reflects the cultural values of individualism and dislike of government, and for some it reflects judgments about people who are "different." This can shape preferences about laws, policies, and programs affecting the lives of millions of people. Though some people like to think that racism, sexism, and other forms of discrimination are much less significant today than they were a half century ago, it is more useful to think of them as appearing in public life in different forms.

While African American citizens in an earlier time were prevented from voting or in extreme circumstances beaten or lynched for exercising basic rights, today voting may be made inconvenient or difficult. People years ago may have had relatively little schooling, while today many children in poor neighborhoods attend lower-quality schools than those in more affluent areas. The openly racist expressions of an earlier time have been replaced, for example, by questioning the citizenship of a black U.S. president or by harassment of particular ethnic groups. The absence of adequate government response to the poverty, malnutrition, and deadly working conditions a hundred years ago is replaced by attempts to weaken public programs designed to alleviate some of the more serious effects of economic inequality.

Because there is considerable resistance to dealing with these issues through the public sector, it may be that

> the best we can do is to offer some amelioration through social welfare programs, incremental improvement of schools, and so on. Comprehensive solutions such as investment in urban jobs, schools, training programs, day care, transportation, whatever it takes to solve the problem may today be outside the realm of political will. . . . How Americans have come to accept this reality of contemporary life as unchanging and morally acceptable is an interesting question. (Box 2008, 63)

Resistance to comprehensive social change is, according to George Frederickson (1980, 7), a product of "pluralistic government," which favors bureaucracies and their clientele (such as the Department of Agriculture and large farmers) over minorities such as farm workers. Eventually, "the continuation of widespread unemployment, poverty, disease, ignorance, and hopelessness in an era of economic growth" may result in social unrest which is "a fundamental, if long range, threat to the viability of this or any political system" (7).

Though many public policies are not as effective as we would like, without public sector involvement inequality, inequity, and injustice would be much, much more serious and troubling than they are today. Also, it is not only the people who create policy by passing laws who have an effect on social equity. According to Johnson and Svara (2011a, 5), "Often problems are identified and policies are recommended by administrators. Furthermore, given the nature of American political values and the incremental expansion of justice and equality, advances often occur through administrative actions within the existing policy framework rather than dramatic policy change."

When public professionals are aware of inequitable conditions, they may feel a responsibility to take appropriate action. This is an example of applying McCollough's ethical question in daily practice by asking "What is my personal relation to what I know?"

Johnson and Svara (2011b, 286) think that "public administrators must be attentive to new expressions of the social inequality challenge and creative in combating these inequalities." They believe public professionals should emphasize fairness and equity (solving the problem of low-quality schools in poorer neighborhoods is illustrative) (277) and they draw from Richard Box (1998) in suggesting that everyone who wishes to participate in public life should "have a place at the table when needs are identified, policy options discussed, and programs and services assessed" (Johnson and Svara 2011b, 278).

Social Equity in Practice: The Missing Sidewalks

Here is a real-life illustration of an opportunity for a public professional to advance social equity in a common practice situation. In this case, the opportunity was missed. As part of a state-funded study of neighborhoods in a medium-sized city of about 300,000 residents, I found that in one area there were no sidewalks near an elementary school. In this lower-income neighborhood, children were walking to school on the sides of traffic lanes in busy streets. There had been no serious accidents to date resulting from this situation, but it seemed to be a matter of time. The city public works director allocated equal portions of infrastructure improvement funds to each district from which council members were elected, so wealthy areas with good infrastructure received the same level of funding as poorer areas with inadequate infrastructure. After other improvement needs were met in this neighborhood, there were no funds available to build new sidewalks near the school.

When I asked the public works director about the situation, he said that council members would be upset if their districts did not receive their "fair share," so he was not going to raise the issue. Had he wished to advocate for policy change, he could have discussed the problem with the city manager and the mayor and/ or council. He could have talked with neighborhood groups and community leaders to explore possible support for change. He could have recommended forming a citizen's advisory board for capital projects to study a range of issues, including allocation of infrastructure improvement funds. He could have declared a safety emergency and reallocated funds on his own authority.

I did not follow up in later years to discover whether anything had been done about this situation and the broader question of resource equity and social justice in this city; it may be that significant progress has been made, or maybe not. For our purposes, this situation was ripe for advocacy, applying professional knowledge in the public interest and serving the value of social equity. This sort of inequity is common at the local level. In areas occupied by low-income or minority residents, it is not unusual to find poor-quality schools, deteriorating infrastructure, abuses or neglect by law enforcement personnel, few and/or dangerous parks and open spaces, inadequate attention to housing conditions, and many other problems related to public services.

This case illustrates the possibilities and the barriers to applying the value of social equity in daily practice. It would be easy to argue that installing a sidewalk in this neighborhood was in the public interest, in the interest of not only the residents in the immediate area, but residents of the city as a whole. City staff knew about this situation, so if a child walking in the street was involved in an accident, the city could face liability for failure to act in a safe and professionally acceptable manner. Social equity may not be the primary value on the minds of most practitioners as they go about their work. However, since it is directly related to current public affairs and politics and since the degree of inequality in the United States is increasing, it seems worthwhile for us to consider it as a critical issue of policy and practice.

Applying the Value of Public Interest in Professional Life

The public interest is many things, but in this chapter we have explored how it can serve as a central organizing theme for public service professionals who have a commitment to making a difference. Making a difference was discussed in Chapter 6 as a personal commitment, and the public interest is a way to think about what changes public professionals want to bring about in society. As a seemingly small part of a large system, we may not be aware of our contribution to the public interest, but even if we are not involved in high-visibility public issues we can impact policies and practices that are important to the people we serve.

Participativeness, representativeness, transparency, and social equity help draw together value themes of democracy, pluralism, imagination, fairness, empathy, and others discussed in *Public Service Values*, applying them to the idea that seeking the public interest is an important, worthwhile part of public service. Terry Cooper (2012, 81) writes, "The function served by the concept of public interest is not so much one of defining specifically what we ought to do or even providing operational criteria for particular decision-making problems. Rather the public interest stands as a kind of question mark before all decisions and conduct." We may never achieve exactly what we think is the public interest, but the process of trying to identify it is of value in itself, bringing people together to imagine a better future.

8

Conclusion

Value Choices and the Public Professional

VALUES IN PRACTICE

Our exploration of public service values shows that they can help in understanding the actions of public professionals and provide a useful framework for decision making. They are one of a number of perspectives on administrative behavior, not the only one or necessarily the best, but valuable (pun intended!) and worth our time and attention. Public service values are a quite specific sort of values; thus, the focus of this discussion has been the workplace setting of career public professionals.

Chapters on neutrality, efficiency, and accountability have drawn on important concepts in public affairs to examine the role of the public professional in a democratic society. We find a role bounded by legal and institutional constraints and public expectations, and also rich with public purpose and a tradition of public service. The chapters on public service and public interest move beyond the historical and institutional setting to explore personal commitments and ways of thinking about the broader public good.

The context of this discussion has been the place of public service in a society characterized by cultural skepticism about the collective decision making and action of government. In part because of the influence of private interests on the public sector, this is a challenging environment that often tests the value commitments of public professionals. The key point is that the societal environment matters to public service: historical development and events, institutional structures, unique national cultures, public attitudes and expectations, and trends and changes in economics and politics all play their part in shaping public service and public organizations.

The five values used here to organize the discussion are not the only ones we might have chosen, but they focus attention on key issues in the practice of public service. Though they cannot by themselves lead people to a single, "right" decision or action, they offer a framework for reflecting on the reasons for acting and the sort of future we want to create.

IMAGINATION, EMPATHY, AND THE PUBLIC INTEREST

From neutral implementer of public policy to active agent of social change, public professionals have a variety of role options from which to choose. The discussion in *Public Service Values* is about roles and behaviors defined by the constitutional, legal, and organizational boundaries of legitimate action. On occasion, public professionals choose to go outside these boundaries by taking actions that violate existing policies or going to the public with their concerns (whistle-blowing). Important as these actions can be in specific situations, they are relatively uncommon and we have not focused on them.

That said, within the accepted boundaries of the professional role, people who choose public service as a career can have significant impacts on society, "making a difference" in important and constructive ways. The idea of public interest can be used as a tool for imagining possible changes in policies and practices that would produce beneficial results for the people we serve. In a society in which injustice, inequity, lack of opportunity, and suffering are all too common, public professionals can use empathy to imagine the life experiences of others, crafting proposals, actions, and solutions intended to make the future better than the present.

PUBLIC SERVICE VALUES ACROSS CULTURES

As noted above, the societal environment matters to public service and to public service values, shaping and influencing them in many ways. *Public Service Values* is written in the American cultural context, but with the understanding, the hope, that it may be useful to people in other places who want to explore the interactions between values and actions in public service. This is more than a suggestion that cross-national research on public service values can provide interesting comparisons that increase our understanding of values and cultures. Certainly this is important, but thinking beyond the familiar and the comfortable can also yield insights that may lead to changes in our own public service practices.

One example would be the relationship between values and market-based management techniques. This is the focus of discussion in Chapter 4, illustrated with the case study of a fictional city, Vacation Beach, Florida. The case study explores the value trade-offs involved in reorganizing operations around a particular value orientation, and, of course, it does so within the specifically American context. However, what sort of differences would we find if the case were reframed within the societal environments of other countries? What would the results say about the values people care about in those societies, and would market-oriented values prove to be compatible with the broader cultural context?

If Americans and people in other countries use the public service values perspective to examine their practices and to compare them with those in other countries, will they find inconsistencies and imbalances that suggest the need for a change in assumptions, areas that are overemphasized or slighted given current value commitments? It can be difficult to take time from our busy schedules to think about values and practices at this level of abstraction, but the potential for productive change would seem to make the effort worthwhile.

QUESTIONS ABOUT PUBLIC SERVICE VALUES IN PRACTICE

There are many public service values, and choosing when and how to use specific values can be complicated. *Public Service*

Values offers a point of entry into a particular perspective on public service, a point of beginning rather than a comprehensive exploration. Though it is a beginning, the book's discussion is sufficiently detailed that it would be difficult to summarize it in this concluding chapter. Instead, we can think about questions that may draw us into the public service values perspective and encourage us to apply it in everyday affairs.

The preface ends with the hope that this book "will contribute to a more conscious and reflective public practice." I would add to this a wish that readers will find their professional lives enriched by this exploration of public service values. The questions below are intended as tools for putting these values into practice.

Whom Do I Serve, and for What Purposes?

This question immediately focuses our attention on the public service value *accountability*. In the process of sorting out what people or groups are supported by our efforts, we can more clearly identify which values are served by our actions and whether some important values are being ignored or given too little weight.

What Is My Personal Relation to What I Know?

Thomas McCollough's (1991) perceptive question pushes us to take responsibility for conditions we know about, seeking to change things for the better.

What Public Service Values Are Emphasized in the Particular Decision, Event, Policy, or Practice That I Am Thinking About Today?

Being aware of the public service values perspective is not the same thing as putting it into practice. This question prompts us to use the values perspective in routine daily settings, not only with big issues or transitions.

What Values Are Slighted or Minimized in a Particular Situation That Might Be Important to the People Involved, to Outcomes, and to Future Conditions?

There are often value trade-offs present in a given issue or problem-solving situation. Identification of values being used explicitly or implicitly can lead to thinking about whether some values should be given greater weight.

Can I Improve on My Understanding of the Circumstances Surrounding a Particular Situation by Using Imagination and Empathy?

Using imagination as a technique in support of problem solving and decision making can be a powerful way to increase the effectiveness of professional action. Empathy supports the use of values and imagination in decision making by encouraging us to think about the circumstances other people are experiencing. This can strengthen our determination to treat them with dignity, compassion, and our full attention.

Given What I Know About Public Service Values, Are There Policies, Practices, or Programs That Might Be Changed in Ways That Better Serve the Values I Think Are Important?

This question is a variation on themes from the questions above that ask what public service values are emphasized and what values are slighted or minimized in a particular situation.

Am I Acting in Ways That Will Serve the Public Interest in the Long Term?

A particular goal or outcome, such as improving quality of life, social equity, or the natural environment, may not be relevant to each public professional, but the overall question is important. It asks whether our actions support the long-term public interest; if not, it may be time to make changes in our values orientation.

References

Allen, W.B., Gordon Lloyd, and Margie Lloyd, eds. 1985. *The Essential Antifederalist*. Lanham, MD: University Press of America.

Alvaredo, Facundo, Anthony B. Atkinson, Thomas Piketty, and Emmanuel Saez. 2013. "The Top 1 Percent in International and Historical Perspective." *Journal of Economic Perspectives* 27 (3): 3–20.

American Planning Association. 2009. "AICP Code of Ethics and Professional Conduct." www.planning.org/ethics/ethicscode.htm.

American Society for Public Administration (ASPA). 2013. "ASPA Code of Ethics." www.aspanet.org/public/ASPA/Resources/Code_of_Ethics/ASPA/Resources/Code%20of%20Ethics1.aspx?hkey=acd40318-a945-4ffc-ba7b-18e037b1a858.

Axelrod, Nancy R. 2005. "Board Leadership and Development." In *The Jossey-Bass Handbook of Nonprofit Leadership and Management*, 2nd ed., edited by Robert D. Herman and Associates, 131–152. San Francisco: Jossey-Bass.

Bachrach, Peter, and Morton S. Baratz. 1962. "Two Faces of Power." *American Political Science Review* 56 (4): 947–952.

Ball, Carolyn. 2009. "What Is Transparency?" *Public Integrity* 11 (4): 293–307.

Bao, Guoxian, Xuejun Wang, Gary L. Larsen, and Douglas F. Morgan. 2012. "Beyond New Public Governance: A Value-Based Global Framework for Performance Management, Governance, and Leadership." *Administration & Society* 45 (4): 443–467.

Behn, Robert D. 2001. *Rethinking Democratic Accountability*. Washington, DC: Brookings Institution Press.

Bellone, Carl J., and George Frederick Goerl. 1992. "Reconciling Public Entrepreneurship and Democracy." *Public Administration Review* 52 (2): 130–134.

Benington, John, and Mark H. Moore. 2011. *Public Value: Theory and Practice*. New York: Palgrave Macmillan.

Box, Richard C. 1998. *Citizen Governance: Leading American Communities into the 21st Century*. Thousand Oaks, CA: Sage.

———. 1999. "Running Government Like a Business: Implications for Public Administration Theory and Practice." *American Review of Public Administration* 29 (1): 19–43.

———. 2005. *Critical Social Theory in Public Administration*. Armonk, NY: M.E. Sharpe.

———. 2007a. "Redescribing the Public Interest." *Social Science Journal* 44 (4): 585–598.

———. 2007b. "The Public Service Practitioner as Agent of Social Change." In *Democracy and Public Administration*, edited by Richard C. Box, 194–211. Armonk, NY: M.E. Sharpe.

———. 2008. *Making a Difference: Progressive Values in Public Administration.* Armonk, NY: M.E. Sharpe.

———. 2011. "The Citizenship Role of the Public Professional: Imagining Private Lives and Alternative Futures." In *Government Is Us 2.0*, edited by Cheryl Simrell King, 59–75. Armonk, NY: M.E. Sharpe.

———. 2014. *Public Administration and Society: Critical Issues in American Governance.* 3rd ed. Armonk, NY: M.E. Sharpe.

Box, Richard C., Gary S. Marshall, B.J. Reed, and Christine M. Reed. 2001. "New Public Management and Substantive Democracy." *Public Administration Review* 61 (5): 608–619.

Bozeman, Barry. 2007. *Public Values and Public Interest: Counterbalancing Economic Individualism.* Washington, DC: Georgetown University Press.

Brewer, Gene A., Sally Coleman Selden, and Rex L. Facer II. 2000. "Individual Conceptions of Public Service Motivation." *Public Administration Review* 60 (3): 254–264.

Coates, Rodney D. 2007. "Social Justice and Pedagogy." *American Behavioral Scientist* 51 (4): 579–591.

Colm, Gerhard. 1962. "The Public Interest: Essential Key to Public Policy." In *The Public Interest*, edited by Carl J. Friedrich, 115–128. New York: Atherton Press.

Cooper, Terry L. 1991. *An Ethic of Citizenship for Public Administration.* Englewood Cliffs, NJ: Prentice Hall.

———. 2012. *The Responsible Administrator: An Approach to Ethics for the Administrative Role.* 6th ed. San Francisco: Jossey-Bass.

Demmke, Christoph, and Timo Moilanen. 2012. *Effectiveness of Public-Service Ethics and Good Governance in the Central Administration of the EU-27: Evaluating Outcomes in the Context of the Financial Crisis.* Frankfurt am Main: Peter Lang.

Denhardt, Janet V., and Robert B. Denhardt. 2011. *The New Public Service: Serving, Not Steering.* 3rd ed. Armonk, NY: M.E. Sharpe.

Frederickson, H. George. 1980. *New Public Administration.* Tuscaloosa: University of Alabama Press.

———. 1997. *The Spirit of Public Administration.* San Francisco: Jossey-Bass.

Gooden, Susan T. 2014. *Race and Social Equity: A Nervous Area of Government.* Armonk, NY: M.E. Sharpe.

Goodsell, Charles T. 1989. "Balancing Competing Values." In *Handbook of Public Administration*, edited by James L. Perry, 575–584. San Francisco: Jossey-Bass.

Gruening, Gernod. 2001. "Origin and Theoretical Basis of New Public Management." *International Public Management Journal* 4 (1): 1–25.

Hamilton, Mary R. 2014. "Democracy and Public Service." In *Public Administration and Society: Critical Issues in American Governance*, 3rd ed., edited by Richard C. Box, 275–287. Armonk, NY: M.E. Sharpe.

Herman, Robert D., and Dick Heimovics. 2005. "Executive Leadership." In *The Jossey-Bass Handbook of Nonprofit Leadership and Management*, 2nd ed., edited by Robert D. Herman and Associates, 153–170. San Francisco: Jossey-Bass.

Herring, E. Pendleton. 1997. "Public Administration and the Public Interest." In *Classics of Public Administration*, 4th ed., edited by Jay M. Shafritz and Albert C. Hyde, 76–80. New York: Harcourt Brace.

International City/County Management Association (ICMA). 2013. "ICMA Code of Ethics with Guidelines." http://icma.org/en/icma/knowledge_network/documents/kn/Document/100265/ICMA_Code_of_Ethics_with_Guidelines.

Irvin, Renee A., and John Stansbury. 2004. "Citizen Participation in Decision Making: Is It Worth the Effort?" *Public Administration Review* 64 (1): 55–65.

Johnson, Norman J., and James H. Svara. 2011a. "Social Equity in American Society and Public Administration." In *Justice for All: Promoting Social Equity in Public Administration*, edited by Norman J. Johnson and James H. Svara, 3–25. Armonk, NY: M.E. Sharpe.

———. 2011b. "Toward a More Perfect Union: Moving Forward with Social Equity." In *Justice for All: Promoting Social Equity in Public Administration*, edited by Norman J. Johnson and James H. Svara, 265–290. Armonk, NY: M.E. Sharpe.

Jørgensen, Torben Beck, and Barry Bozeman. 2007. "Public Values: An Inventory." *Administration & Society* 39 (3): 354–381.

Josephson, Michael. 2006. "The Six Pillars of Character." In *The Ethics Edge*, 2nd ed., edited by Jonathan P. West and Evan M. Berman, 11–17. Washington, DC: ICMA Press.

Judd, Dennis R., and Todd Swanstrom. 2011. *City Politics: The Political Economy of Urban America*. Glenview, IL: Pearson.

Kalu, Kalu N. 2003. "Entrepreneurs or Conservators? Contractarian Principles of Bureaucratic Performance." *Administration & Society* 35 (5): 539–563.

Kennedy, Sheila, and David Schultz. 2011. *American Public Service: Constitutional and Ethical Foundations*. Sudbury, MA: Jones & Bartlett.

Kernaghan, Kenneth. 2003. "Integrating Values into Public Service: The Values Statement as Centerpiece." *Public Administration Review* 63 (6): 711–719.

Killinger, Barbara. 2010. *Integrity: Doing the Right Thing for the Right Reason*. Montreal: McGill-Queen's University Press.

King, Cheryl Simrell, and Renee Rank. 2011. "The Context: Citizens, Administrators, and Their Discontents." In *Government Is Us 2.0*, edited by Cheryl Simrell King, 3–16. Armonk, NY: M.E. Sharpe.

King, Cheryl Simrell, and Lisa A. Zanetti. 2005. *Transformational Public Service: Portraits of Theory in Practice*. Armonk, NY: M.E. Sharpe.

Koliba, Christopher, Jack W. Meek, and Asim Zia. 2011. *Governance Networks in Public Administration and Public Policy*. Boca Raton, FL: CRC Press.

Krugman, Paul. 2007. *The Conscience of a Liberal*. New York: Norton.

Lewis, Carol W. 2006. "In Pursuit of the Public Interest." *Public Administration Review* 66 (5): 694–701.

Lowi, Theodore J. 1969. *The End of Liberalism: Ideology, Policy, and the Crisis of Public Authority*. New York: Norton.

McCollough, Thomas E. 1991. *The Moral Imagination and Public Life: Raising the Ethical Question*. Chatham, NJ: Chatham House.

Meine, Manfred F., and Thomas P. Dunn. 2013. "The Search for Ethical Competency: Do Ethics Codes Matter?" *Public Integrity* 15 (2): 149–166.

Miller, Hugh T., and Charles J. Fox. 2007. *Postmodern Public Administration.* Armonk, NY: M.E. Sharpe.

Molina, Anthony DeForest, and Cassandra L. McKeown. 2012. "The Heart of the Profession: Understanding Public Service Values." *Journal of Public Affairs Education* 18 (2): 375–396.

Moore, Mark H. 1995. *Creating Public Value: Strategic Management in Government.* Cambridge, MA: Harvard University Press.

NASPAA. 2009. "NASPAA Accreditation Standards for Master's Degree Programs." www.naspaa.org/accreditation/NS/naspaastandards.asp.

Norton, Michael I., and Dan Ariely. 2011. "Building a Better America—One Wealth Quintile at a Time." *Perspectives on Psychological Science* 6 (1): 9–12.

Oakerson, Ronald J. 1989. "Governance Structures for Enhancing Accountability and Responsiveness." In *Handbook of Public Administration*, edited by James L. Perry, 114–130. San Francisco: Jossey-Bass.

O'Flynn, Janine. 2007. "From New Public Management to Public Value: Paradigmatic Change and Managerial Implications." *Australian Journal of Public Administration* 66 (3): 353–366.

O'Leary, Rosemary. 2014. *The Ethics of Dissent: Managing Guerrilla Government.* 2nd ed. Thousand Oaks, CA: CQ Press.

Organisation for Economic Co-operation and Development (OECD). 2010. "A Family Affair: Intergenerational Social Mobility Across OECD Countries." In *Economic Policy Reforms 2010: Going for Growth*, 183–200. Paris: OECD.

Osborne, David, and Ted Gaebler. 1993. *Reinventing Government: How the Entrepreneurial Spirit Is Transforming the Public Sector.* New York: Penguin Books.

Osborne, Stephen P., ed. 2010. *The New Public Governance? Emerging Perspectives on the Theory and Practice of Public Governance.* London: Routledge.

Perry, James L., Annie Hondeghem, and Lois Recascino Wise. 2010. "Revisiting the Motivational Bases of Public Service: Twenty Years of Research and an Agenda for the Future." *Public Administration Review* 70 (5): 681–690.

Perry, James L., and Lois Recascino Wise. 1990. "The Motivational Bases of Public Service." *Public Administration Review* 50 (3): 367–373.

Quinn, Frederick, ed. 1993. *The Federalist Papers Reader.* Washington, DC: Seven Locks Press.

Redford, Emmette S. 1969. *Democracy and the Administrative State.* New York: Oxford University Press.

Rohr, John A. 1989. *Ethics for Bureaucrats: An Essay on Law and Values.* 2nd ed. New York: Marcel Dekker.

Romzek, Barbara S., and Melvin J. Dubnick. 1987. "Accountability in the Public Sector: Lessons from the *Challenger* Tragedy." *Public Administration Review* 47 (3): 227–238.

Rorty, Richard. 1999. *Philosophy and Social Hope.* London: Penguin Books.

Rosenbloom, David H. 2003. *Administrative Law for Public Managers.* Boulder, CO: Westview Press.

Rutgers, Mark R. 2008. "Sorting Out Public Values? On the Contingency of Value Classifications in Public Administration." *Administrative Theory & Praxis* 30 (1): 92–113.

Schachter, Hindy Lauer. 1997. *Reinventing Government or Reinventing Ourselves: The Role of Citizen Owners in Making a Better Government*. Albany: State University of New York Press.

Schlesinger, Arthur M. 1986. *The Cycles of American History*. Boston: Houghton Mifflin.

Schubert, Glendon A., Jr. 1957. "The Public Interest in Administrative Decision-Making: Theorem, Theosophy, or Theory?" *American Political Science Review* 51 (2): 346–368.

———. 1960. *The Public Interest: A Critique of the Theory of a Political Concept*. Glencoe, IL: Free Press.

Stillman, Richard J., II. 1991. *Preface to Public Administration: A Search for Themes and Direction*. New York: St. Martin's Press.

Stivers, Camilla M. 1990. "Active Citizenship and Public Administration." In *Refounding Public Administration*, edited by Gary L. Wamsley, Robert N. Bacher, Charles T. Goodsell, Philip S. Kronenberg, John A. Rohr, Camilla M. Stivers, Orion F. White, and James F. Wolf, 246–273. Newbury Park, CA: Sage.

———. 1994. "The Listening Bureaucrat: Responsiveness in Public Administration." *Public Administration Review* 54 (4): 364–369.

Stone, Deborah. 2002. *Policy Paradox: The Art of Political Decision Making*. Rev. ed. New York: Norton.

Stuteville, Rebekkah, and Laurie N. DiPadova-Stocks. 2011. "Advancing and Assessing Public Service Values in Professional Programs: The Case of the Hauptmann School's Master of Public Affairs Program." *Journal of Public Affairs Education* 17 (4): 585–610.

Svara, James H. 2015. *The Ethics Primer for Public Administrators in Government and Nonprofit Organizations*. 2nd ed. Burlington, MA: Jones and Bartlett.

Terry, Larry D. 1993. "Why We Should Abandon the Misconceived Quest to Reconcile Public Entrepreneurship with Democracy." *Public Administration Review* 53 (4): 393–395.

———. 1998. "Administrative Leadership, Neo-Managerialism, and the Public Management Movement." *Public Administration Review* 58 (3): 194–200.

Thomas, John Clayton. 2012. *Citizen, Customer, Partner: Engaging the Public in Public Management*. Armonk, NY: M.E. Sharpe.

Timney, Mary M. 2011. "Models of Citizen Participation: Measuring Engagement and Collaboration." In *Government Is Us 2.0*, edited by Cheryl Simrell King, 86–100. Armonk, NY: M.E. Sharpe.

U.S. Census Bureau. 1992. *1992 Census of Governments*, Volume 1, Number 2, Popularly Elected Officials. www.census.gov/prod/2/gov/gc/gc92_1_2.pdf.

———. 2011a. *2011 Annual Survey of Public Employment and Payroll: Federal Government Civilian Employment*. www2.census.gov/govs/apes/11fedfun.pdf.

———. 2011b. *2011 Public Employment and Payroll Data: Local Governments*. www2.census.gov/govs/apes/11locus.txt.

———. 2011c. *2011 Public Employment and Payroll Data: State Governments*. www2.census.gov/govs/apes/11stus.txt.

Van der Wal, Zeger, and Leo Huberts. 2008. "Value Solidity in Government and Business: Results of an Empirical Study on Public and Private Sector Organizational Values." *American Review of Public Administration* 38 (3): 264–285.

Van Wart, Montgomery. 1998. *Changing Public Sector Values*. New York: Garland.

Waldo, Dwight. 1980. *The Enterprise of Public Administration: A Summary View*. Novato, CA: Chandler & Sharp.

Wamsley, Gary L., Charles T. Goodsell, John A. Rohr, Camilla M. Stivers, Orion F. White, and James F. Wolf. 1987. "The Public Administration and the Governance Process: Refocusing the American Dialogue." In *A Centennial History of the American Administrative State*, edited by Ralph Clark Chandler, 291–317. New York: Free Press.

Whitcombe, Judy. 2008. "Contributions and Challenges of 'New Public Management': New Zealand Since 1984." *Policy Quarterly* 4 (3): 7–13.

Wood, Gordon S. 1969. *The Creation of the American Republic, 1776–1787*. Chapel Hill: University of North Carolina Press.

Yang, Lijing, and Zeger van der Wal. 2014. "Rule of Morality vs. Rule of Law? An Exploratory Study of Civil Servant Values in China and the Netherlands." *Public Integrity* 16 (2): 187–206.

Yankelovich, Daniel. 1991. *Coming to Public Judgment: Making Democracy Work in a Complex World*. Syracuse, NY: Syracuse University Press.

Zanetti, Lisa A. 2011. "Cultivating and Sustaining Empathy as a Normative Value in Public Administration." In *Government Is Us 2.0*, edited by Cheryl Simrell King, 76–85. Armonk, NY: M.E. Sharpe.

Index

A

accountability
  bureaucratic, 96
  in contracting and budgeting, 88
  legal, 96
  political, 97
  professional, 9–10, 96, 166
  theme of, xii, 21
administrative discretion, 59–60
Administrative Procedure Act, 63
Age of Enlightenment, 16, 61
Allen, W.B., 16
Alvaredo, Facundo, 123
American Institute of Certified Planners, 37
American Planning Association, 37, 38
American Society for Public
  Administration, 24
Ariely, Dan, 123–124
Articles of Confederation, 61
ASPA Code of Ethics, 39–41
Axelrod, Nancy R., 126

B

Bachrach, Peter, 154
Ball, Carolyn, 113
Bao, Guoxian, 7
Baratz, Morton S., 154
Behn, Robert D., 101
Bellone, Carl J., 91
Benington, John, 6
Box, Richard C., 5, 6, 34, 35, 36, 61, 83,
  92, 122, 128, 136, 143, 149–150,
  151, 153–154, 159, 160
Bozeman, Barry, 6, 12, 21, 23–24,
  42, 146

branch manager, the, 142–143
Brewer, Gene A., 28–29

C

citizen involvement, 19, 34–35, 105–106,
  138–139, 151
citizens in lieu of the rest of us, 35–36
classical liberalism, 61
classical republicanism, 61
Coates, Rodney D., 156
Colm, Gerhard, 145
comparative research, xiii, 164–165
competition, 80
Constitution, U.S., 16, 60–62, 99–100,
  114
constitutional ethic, 61
contracted public services, 13, 88
Cooper, Terry L., 35–36, 62, 107–110,
  112, 134–135, 144, 162
customer-driven government, 91–93
customers and owners, 87–88

D

Declaration of Independence, 16
Demmke, Christoph, 72
democracy
  direct, 33
  governance and, 116
  inequality and, 123
  loop model of, 102
  overhead, 101
  public service and, 120
  representative, 33, 53, 102
Denhardt, Janet V., 6, 62, 63, 80, 83, 116,
  147

Denhardt, Robert B., 6, 62, 63, 80, 83,
     116, 147
DiPadova-Stocks, Laurie N., 29–30
dissent, in organizations, 111
Dubnick, Melvin J., 96–97
Dunn, Thomas P., 37
duty, 115

E
economic perspective, 81–83
economics and metropolitan areas,
     82–83
effectiveness, 113
efficiency, xii, 9, 21
elected leaders, 7–8
empathy, 140–141, 164, 167
entrepreneurial, 80, 91
environment, societal, xii–xiii, 15–18,
     119–121, 128–130
ethics
   administrative, xi, 30–32, 107
   Code of, American Institute of Certified
      Planners, 37–39
   Code of, American Society for Public
      Administration, 39–41
   Code of, International City/County
      Management Association, 64
   Practices to promote the ASPA Code of,
      46–50
   virtue, principle, and consequences,
      31–32
expertise, 69–70
external concepts, 118

F
Facer, Rex L. II, 28–29
failure of representation, 66–68
fairness, 88–89
Federalist Papers, The, 121
Finer, Herman, 62, 63
five primary themes, xii
flexible budgeting process, 88
Founding Era, 129
Fox, Charles J., 102
Frederickson, H. George, 5, 97, 159
Freedom of Information Act, 153
Friedrich, Carl, 63

G
Gaebler, Ted, 5, 80, 83, 90–91
Gilded Age, 76, 123, 158
Goerl, George Frederick, 91
Gooden, Susan T., 158
Goodsell, Charles T., 18, 27
governance network, 6–7, 115–116
Great Depression, 76
Great Society, 76
Gruening, Gernod, 81

H
Hamilton, Alexander, 121
Hamilton, Mary R., 120
helper role, 35, 153–154
Herring, E. Pendleton, 144–145
Hondeghem, Annie, 118
honesty, 9
Huberts, Leo, 23
human behavior, 121–123

I
imagination, 152, 164, 167
imagining alternative futures, 139–140,
     152
imagining private lives, 36, 152
impartiality, 70–71
Industrial Revolution, 52
inequality, 123–125
innovativeness, 91
inside perspective, 10
integrity, 118–119, 130–135
intergenerational mobility, 124–125
internal concepts, 118
International City/County Management
     Association (ICMA), 64

J
Jay, John, 121
Jefferson, Thomas, 61
Johnson, Norman J., 157–158, 159–160
Jørgensen, Torben Beck, 21, 23–24
Josephson, Michael, 31
Judd, Dennis R., 52

K
Kalu, Kalu N., 103

Kennedy, Sheila, 60–61, 99
Kernaghan's categories of public service
  values, *28*
Kernaghan, Kenneth, 21, 24, 27–28,
  42–43
Killinger, Barbara, 130–131
King, Cheryl Simrell, 75, 135
Koliba, Christopher, 6–7, 83
Krugman, Paul, 75

L

lawfulness, 9, 100
legitimacy, administrative, 19
Lewis, Carol W., 147
Lippmann, Walter, 144
listening bureaucrat, 35
Lloyd, Gordon, 16
Lloyd, Margie, 16
Lowi, Theodore J., 62
loyalty, 69

M

Madison, James, 75, 114, 121–122
making a difference, 119, 135–136, 161,
  164
McCollough, Thomas E., 70, 135, 140,
  159
McKeown, Cassandra L., 10, 24–25, 73,
  95, 113
Meek, Jack W., 6–7, 83
Meine, Manfred F., 37
Micro, City of, 107–110, 111, 114–115,
  116, 131
Miller, Hugh T., 102
missing sidewalks, the, 160–161
mixed economy, 17
Moilanen, Timo, 72
Molina, Anthony DeForest, 10, 24–25, 73,
  95, 113
Moore, Mark H., 6

N

national parks, 84–85
network environment, 97
Network of Schools of Public Policy,
  Affairs, and Administration
  (NASPAA), 41–43

neutrality, 4, 21, 51
new, as a concept, 20–21
New Deal, 76
New Public Administration, 4–5
New Public Governance, 7
New Public Management, 4, 6, 79, 84–90
nodal values, 21
nonprofit board of directors, 126–127
nonprofit sector, 125–126
Norton, Michael I., 123–124

O

Oakerson, Ronald J., 95–96
obedience, 69
O'Flynn, Janine, 79–80
O'Leary, Rosemary, 111
organizational expectations, 64–65
Osborne, David, 5, 7, 80, 83, 90–91

P

packages of services, 82
Park Woods, 131–135
participativeness, 87–88
performance measurement, 89
Perry, James L., 117–118
pillars of character, six, 31
pluralism, 89, 105
political appointees, 8
political machines, 52
politics and administration, 4, 54–58
POSDCORB, 78
post-NPM era, 79
PPBS, 78
private interest and public purpose, 18,
  74–78, 120–121
profitability, 9, 87, 90–91
Progressive Era, 34, 52–53, 76, 158
public interest
  and accountability, 110–112
  aggregate perspective of, 146
  and economics, 81–85
  and participativeness, 147–150
  and personal transformation, 150
  and time, 149–150
  as a theme, xii, 21
  process perspective of, 146–147
  substantive perspective of, 147

public professionals (public service
  practitioners), 8–9
public sector, 10–11, 14
public service, xii, 21
public service motivation, 117–118

Q
Quinn, Frederick, 16

R
racism, 158–159
Rank, Renee, 75
Reagan, Ronald, 5, 79
Redford, Emmette S., 101
rehearsal of defenses, 134
reinventing government, 5, 80, 90
representativeness, 9, 150–152
responsiveness, 87
Roaring Twenties, 76
Rohr, John A., 61, 99
role conflict, 107, 111
role differences, budgeting example of,
  55–58
roles, 59–60, 107–109
Romzek, Barbara S., 96–97
Rorty, Richard, 122
Rosenbloom, David H., 31–32, 99
running government like a business, 6
Rutgers, Mark R., 20

S
Schlesinger, Arthur M., 18, 75
Schubert, Glendon A., Jr., 145
Schultz, David, 60–61, 99
Selden, Sally Coleman, 28–29
separation of powers, 33
social democracy, 77, 158
social equity, 4, 157–161
social justice, 89
Stillman, Richard J. II, 17
Stivers, Camilla, 35, 148–149
Stone, Deborah, 145–146, 149, 154
Stuteville, Rebekkah, 29–30
surplus, 87
Svara, James H., 30–32, 53, 72, 112, 115,
  157–158, 159–160

Swanstrom, Todd, 52
Sweden, income distribution in, 124

T
Taylor, Frederick Winslow, 101
Terry, Larry D., 83–84, 91
Thomas, John Clayton, 34, 105, 148
Timney, Mary M., 105
transparency, 87, 113–115, 152–155
transparency and the traffic engineer, 155

U
utilitarian measure of outcomes, 32

V
Vacation Beach, City of, 85–90, 165
values
  China, 26–27
  conflict between professional and
    organizational, 133–135
  Confucian, 26–27
  definitions of, 12, 43–45
  Netherlands, 26–27
  occupational specificity, 14, 64
  public service, 13
Van der Wal, Zeger, 23, 26–27
Van Wart, Montgomery, 18, 27

W
Waldo, Dwight, 70, 98, 101
Wamsley, Gary L., 19
Weber, Max, 101
whistleblowing, 112
Whitcombe, Judy, 81
Wilson, Woodrow, 101
Wise, Lois Recascino, 117–118
Wood, Gordon S., 16

Y
Yang, Lijing, 26–27
Yankelovich, Daniel, 70

Z
Zanetti, Lisa A., 135, 140–141
ZBB, 78
Zia, Asim, 6–7, 83

About the Author

Richard C. Box worked in local government for thirteen years before completing his doctorate at the University of Southern California. He has taught at University of Colorado at Colorado Springs, University of Nebraska at Omaha, and Park University, and his writing focuses on the interaction between public service professionals and their political and economic environment. He is the author or editor of *Public Administration and Society: Critical Issues in American Governance*, 3rd ed. (M.E. Sharpe 2014); *Making a Difference: Progressive Values in Public Administration* (M.E. Sharpe 2008); *Democracy and Public Administration* (M.E. Sharpe 2007); *Critical Social Theory in Public Administration* (M.E. Sharpe 2005); and *Citizen Governance: Leading American Communities into the 21st Century* (Sage 1998).